tificial Intelligence
Programming
with Turbo Prolog®

Keith Weiskamp
Terry Hengl

John Wiley & Sons, Inc.
York • Chichester • Brisbane • Toronto • Singapore

Publisher: Stephen Kippur
Editor: Therese A. Zak
Managing Editor: Ruth Greif
Electronic Production Services: Publishers Network

Turbo Pascal is a registered trademark of Borland Interna
IBM PC is a registered trademark of International Busine
  Corporation
Macintosh is a trademark of Apple Computer, Inc.
SpinPro is a trademark of Beckman Instruments, Inc.
Line Expert is a trademark of Concept Development Syste

This publication is designed to provide accurate and autho
information in regard to the subject matter covered. It is s
understanding that the publisher is not engaged in render
accounting, or other professional service. If legal advice or
assistance is required, the service of a competent professio
should be sought. FROM A DECLARATION OF PRINCIP
JOINTLY ADOPTED BY A COMMITTEE OF THE AMEF
ASSOCIATION AND A COMMITTEE OF PUBLISHERS.

Library of Congress Cataloging-in-Publication Data

Weiskamp, Keith.
  Artificial intelligence programming with Turbo Prolog.
  1. Artificial intelligence—Data processing. 2. Turbo
Prolog (Computer program) I. Hengl, Terry. II. Title.
Q336.W45 1988   006.3   87–7347
ISBN 0-471-62752-6

Printed in the United States of America
88 89 10 9 8 7 6 5 4 3 2 1

Preface

In less than two years, Borland International's Turbo Prolog® has grown from a new language, struggling for its identity, to an established AI language with over 100,000 users. In fact, Turbo Prolog is now the most used version of the Prolog language. Unfortunately, very few books have been written to show readers how to get beyond the basics of the user's manual. If you're like most readers interested in developing AI applications, you want a book that explains the important concepts of AI and provides realistic programming examples, not just another rewrite of the user's manual.

To fill the gap, this book has two parallel goals: to teach the fundamental concepts of AI programming and to show how Turbo Prolog can be used to write useful, serious programs. Languages are tools for creative thinking and problem solving. Of course, Turbo Prolog is no exception. In addition, its low cost, high performance, and wide user base make Turbo Prolog an excellent language for developing AI applications. We hope that this book helps you unlock many of the mysteries of AI programming with Turbo Prolog.

Who Should Read this Book

Anyone who is interested in developing both their AI and Prolog programming skills should find this book a valuable asset. But if you are a newcomer to AI programming, don't be scared away by the term "artificial intelligence." In many ways, AI is the most humanistic area of computer use.

The material covered in this book is presented in a readable style. Key terms and concepts are introduced with examples to help you to understand the important issues. Both the novice and experienced programmer should benefit from the material and presentation.

What this Book Has to Offer

Artificial Intelligence Programming with Turbo Prolog is written for programmers who are interested in learning about developing AI applications with Turbo Prolog. The major features include:

A practical, hands-on approach to AI programming

Numerous code examples of AI applications from natural language processing to expert systems

A methodical "software tools" approach to developing Turbo Prolog programs

Techniques for developing advanced Turbo Prolog programs

To a large extent, programming with Turbo Prolog requires a new orientation toward problem-solving techniques. This book provides the environment to help you get up to speed with the issues involved in Turbo Prolog programming. Of course, a basic knowledge about the PC and the Prolog language is a prerequisite if you are to get the most out of this book.

Organization

The book is divided into seven chapters, with each covering an aspect of artificial intelligence, Turbo Prolog programming, or both. In the first chapter, you'll be introduced to the world of AI. This chapter will give you an idea about the types of applications that can be developed with Turbo Prolog. To illustrate Turbo Prolog capabilities, procedural (third-generation) languages are compared with Turbo Prolog. This comparison can be extremely useful for experienced third-generation programmers who are trying to "get a handle" on declarative programming principles.

The second chapter discusses some of the basics you'll need to master before moving on to develop useful AI applications: unification, the resolution principle, representing facts and rules, and backtracking. Numerous programming examples are used throughout to demonstrate the important topics. Chapter 3 will get you started in developing Turbo Prolog tools, some of which are used in later chapters for serious program development. The tool approach to program development is very important and unfortunately it is often overlooked in Prolog texts. The presentation in this chapter should greatly assist you in learning about both AI and Turbo Prolog programming in a logical and incremental manner. This is certainly preferable to the "groping in the dark" approach to learning that often results when you rely on user's manuals and reference books.

Chapters 4 through 7 cover the essentials of programming AI applications from natural language processing to expert system development. Chapter 4 presents the techniques involved in logic programming and developing inference engines. Here you will learn, through the programming examples, how to construct a simple inference engine and, in turn, will observe several features of Turbo Prolog "in action." Chapter 5 introduces natural language processing techniques such as recursive transition networks and augmented transition networks. The coded examples provided in this chapter are designed to encourage experimentation. That is, you can modify the examples to study some of the different ways in which natural language programming concepts are applied.

In Chapter 6, techniques for knowledge representation are presented. Topics discussed include characteristics of knowledge, knowledge bases, rules, frames, scripts, and the use of logic to represent facts and relationships. Chapter 7 concludes the book with a discussion about developing expert systems. Extensive programming examples are given throughout the chapter. Expert system development is already a popular AI area, and its scope continues to widen as users uncover new application areas. Thus, the book closes with techniques for developing rule-based, general-purpose expert systems in Turbo Prolog to help you get started.

Starting the AI Adventure

This book presents a lot of material on both programming with Turbo Prolog and artificial intelligence. The book begins with easier concepts and progresses to more advanced topics. The example programs should be tried out whenever possible.

By the way, feel free to experiment with and modify any of the programs included in this book. AI is an area of computer programming that thrives on exploration. Welcome to the next frontier!

Contents

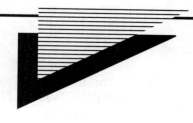

CHAPTER 1

Opening the AI Window

Artificial intelligence is part of the
grand attempt to understand thinking.
—Roger Schank and Larry Hunter
in Byte magazine

A distinctive aspect of intelligence is
the ability to solve new, different problems.
—Marvin Minsky

Getting a Perspective on AI

The fact that you are reading this page means you want to know more about artificial intelligence programming or Turbo Prolog®, or both. To get a quick perspective on artificial intelligence applications today, consider this scenario: You are in charge of route scheduling and bookings for Great Laker Airlines. This morning, you come to work and find your staff panic-stricken. Flights 45, 49, and 53 out of Detroit have been grounded due to a storm. Flights 59, 101, and 23—all destined for Detroit—have been rerouted to a nearby airport, where connecting flight arrangements will have to be made for stranded passengers. And then one of your route managers delivers the really bad news: forty-five employees from your Detroit reservations and ticketing staff have called in sick with a new Midwest flu strain.

You've had bad days before, but this—well, let's just say seven days and nights in Tahiti look pretty good to you now.

It's going to be a long, long day. Now consider how the morning might go if you had given the go-ahead to develop SMART RESERVATIONS, a new reservation and scheduling expert system to be written in Turbo Prolog. Facts and rules about flights for Detroit and all connecting cities would reside, ready for use, in the system's knowledge base. As part of the system, scheduling information for all employees would be built into this program.

Now when your staff tells you about today's Detroit disaster, you remain calm and in control. All you need to do is enter the desired goals in your SMART RESERVATIONS expert system, and it proceeds to find potential solutions for your scheduling problems. The system determines the most efficient way to reschedule flights in and out of Detroit. The program takes into account all existing delays and connecting flight requirements. In addition, SMART RESERVATIONS determines which employees in nearby cities you should contact first to replace your flu-ridden staff. The system considers which cities have the lightest flight schedule loads in proportion to the number of employees available.

You can even instruct your employees on how to use SMART RESERVATIONS. The program is user friendly enough to accommodate novices. Instead of suffering through a crisis, you can now relax and concentrate on getting other important things done.

Expert systems represent only one of many dozen types of applications for artificial intelligence programs. You probably are interested in this book because you have purchased or plan to purchase Turbo Prolog. The odds are that the user's manual provided with the package doesn't answer most of the questions you have about artificial intelligence programming. AI is an exciting field, in part because it provides many creative challenges for programmers. If you program and want to get involved in artificial intelligence, then this book will help you get started.

Exploring and using artificial intelligence programming concepts is the main purpose of this book. In the following chapters, you will use the Turbo Prolog language to explore several realistic artificial intelligence programming applications and concepts such as expert systems, natural language processing programs, and knowledge representations. The Turbo Prolog system is an excellent programming environment for exploring AI applications. Its speed and flexibility make it an ideal language for many programming applications, and its advanced high-level problem solving capabilities make it well suited for writing complex programs.

Understanding the Term: Artificial Intelligence

In recent years, definition of the term *artificial intelligence* (AI) has been a cause for debate among researchers. Numerous computer experts and futurists have volunteered definitions. And you can be sure that the definition offered by one expert will differ from that offered by another expert. Some observers even argue that there is no such thing as artificial intelligence. If it's artificial, they say, then it's not intelligent.

Although an all-encompassing definition of artificial intelligence seems elusive, one thing is certain: the field of artificial intelligence is with us to stay and promises to offer some profound changes in the way that we think and work. In the past, computers were used chiefly to assist people in solving problems and making decisions. These computers mostly performed the task of processing large amounts of numerical data. With current AI hardware and software, on the other hand, people can direct computers to do the actual problem solving and decision making. Many people also use the term AI to refer to computer systems that perform basic physical tasks that once required humans. The use of robots and vision systems in manufacturing applications are two general examples.

You might wonder, then, whether AI will revive the decades-old question:

```
Are computers replacing people?
```

The answer: Current AI technology can handle only a small fraction of the thinking jobs and physical tasks that people perform daily. The ability of computers to think and behave as intelligently as a five-year-old, much less an adult, is little more than a research dream. Machine intelligence pales by comparison with real human intelligence. Thus, the intelligence of even the smartest computers is, without a doubt, limited.

But the real part of the excitement of AI, especially AI programming, is applying the thinking techniques which people use. The computer should be instructed to solve problems much in the way people do. In order to program computers to simulate the ways in which people solve problems, it is important to have a good programming tool—a good programming language. And that's where Turbo Prolog comes in. Traditional programming, on the other hand, is oriented mostly toward numerical problems and programmers must work with primitive logic in order to write programs. Any programmer attempting to construct complex logic in a traditional language will quickly become bogged down in implementation details.

In writing AI programs, the basic goal is to get the computer to simulate some form of human reasoning. Often this task means that the programmer has to describe all parts of a problem area, or domain, to the computer. Of course with a powerful language such as Turbo Prolog, the work of describing problems is made much easier.

Practical AI

A little more than a decade ago, many artificial intelligence programs were considered to be interesting, but not very practical. After all, a business executive doesn't have much use for a program that plays chess or solves a logic puzzle. Early AI research may have seemed trivial to most people, but recent developments prove artificial intelligence is useful and practical. Consider the current AI application areas discussed in the sections to follow. (See Figure 1.1.)

Computer Aided Instruction

In the late 1970s and early 1980s, educators throughout the world began introducing microcomputers into schools. Many administrators and teachers believed these small machines to be the best thing to happen to the classroom since the overhead projector. Educators certainly were correct in their belief that the computer could be a valuable aid to classroom learning. However they were a bit premature in their software expectations.

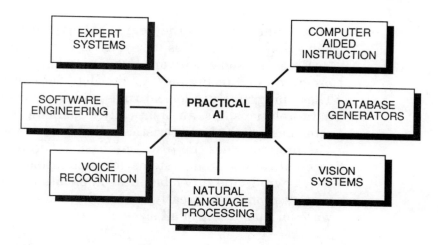

Figure 1.1 Overview of AI Applications

Vendors quickly introduced numerous programs that performed computer aided instruction (CAI). But too many CAI programs look and function alike. In these programs, the computer acts more like a drill-and-practice instructor than a bona fide teacher: the computer asks a question, the student answers, the computer indicates whether the response is correct and perhaps provides a hint. This formula has been used—overused—in literally hundreds of educational programs.

The application of AI in CAI promises to change all that. With intelligent CAI programs, the computer can diagnose each student's current level of understanding. The program also determines the rate at which a student can learn new material and can tailor the instruction to each student's ability. What's more, as natural language and voice recognition systems improve, CAI programs will be able to listen and respond to students in conversational English. With computers assisting students more intelligently, teachers can use their expertise to provide special attention to individual students.

Database Generators

As you may know, a database is a structured collection of data that can be used to support several applications. In the past, the structures of a database had to be designed in great detail on paper. Developing large-scale database systems in this manner requires the help of experts, months of development time, and needless to say, is very expensive.

Recently, some software companies have begun to use AI programming techniques to develop database generators. These programs use logical rules and relationships to create data relationships automatically. Users need only specify some basic data characteristics called frames and dimensions. The program does the rest. Database generators can be used to create integrated systems for accounting, inventory control, payroll, and other business applications. Database generators promise to greatly reduce the cost of developing software for businesses of all sizes.

Vision Systems

Vision systems provide a good example of the problems inherent in simulating basic human activities. When you take a walk in your neighborhood, your eyes and brain work together to form a complex vision system. You recognize and differentiate between objects; you determine the relative speed of moving objects; and you evaluate textures (smooth, rough, glossy, transparent, and so on). You do all this without any apparent conscious thought.

Although vision seems automatic to us, it is a nearly impossible task for machines. For example, getting a machine to grasp one—and only one—small object from among thousands in a box is extremely difficult for current vision systems. The millions of random coordinates that the machine must distinguish between are just too overwhelming. But a child could perform the same task without a second thought.

Even so, operational computer vision systems are successful within limited domains. These systems use the feedback of sensors that determine coordinates as well as symbolic data, such as lines and circles. A system called VISIONS, developed at the University of Massachusetts, can "see" a three-dimensional color image and redraw it on a two-dimensional screen.

Computer vision is a fascinating and growing area of AI. Current technological advances promise to move vision systems into the forefront of practical AI applications. Programming these systems should prove to be an exciting challenge for at least the next few decades.

Natural Language Processing

Simply put, natural language processing refers to the ability of computers to understand languages that people use in everyday activities. At present, no computer system can understand all the meanings and nuances of the English language. In fact, it is unlikely that computers will ever comprehend English nearly as well as people do. Part of the problem stems from the fact that language understanding often requires personal experience and emotional recognition. For instance, how can a computer understand what it's like to be in love? We might be able to get a computer to recognize the word "love" in the context of a sentence or paragraph. However, it isn't possible to get the computer to empathize with the experience or feeling of being in love.

Even so, many aspects of the English language can be recognized by computers. For example, researchers have programmed computers to understand and paraphrase stories. In some programs the computer can even answer detailed questions about certain facts and events presented in the story.

In a more practical vein, natural language programs can be used to accept database instructions input to a computer in conversational English. For example, with a natural language interface, a business user can enter the following request into a database management system:

```
Get me all of the accounts receivable records that have
overdue balances greater than $100 as of July 30.
```

The computer then would search the database and output the indicated records. At present, practical natural language systems require millions of bytes of computer memory. These restrictions make it difficult to implement useful natural language applications on small computers. However, the memory capabilities of small computers are increasing at rapid rates. If this trend continues, it won't be long before powerful natural language interfaces are available for microcomputer systems.

Voice Recognition

If a computer can understand English statements typed through a keyboard, shouldn't it be able to understand spoken English? This question has been posed and studied by many AI researchers. Today, through the work of programmers, linguists, and other specialists, voice recognition systems are becoming a reality.

One of the biggest problems with voice recognition systems lies in the nature of human speech patterns. That is, no two people pronounce the same word or phrase exactly alike. To determine the sound pattern of a particular word, the computer must be able to take into account such variables as regional dialect. If you grew up in the West, you probably distinctly pronounce the letter r in *car*. However, if you're from Boston or Brooklyn, your pronunciation probably sounds more like "kah." What's more, speech variations occur even within the same region. Thus, the fact that every person has his or her own "voiceprint" causes problems for computerized voice recognition systems. Of course additional problems exist even after the system has been customized for one specific speaker. For example, a cold or physical distress can cause sufficient change in the speaker's pitch to confuse a voice recognition system.

One current solution to the problem is to "teach" the computer how to identify the speech patterns of different users. For example, you might type the word *car* on the keyboard of your computer. Next, you speak the word *car* into a standard microphone which is connected to a computer through a specially designed interface. From that point on, the computer appears to understand what you mean when you say *car*. Over time, you can build up an extensive spoken vocabulary that the computer identifies as your personal speech pattern.

Voice recognition systems are currently in use for applications that involve limited, yet specialized user input. For instance, a medical doctor might get tired of typing in the words *acetylsalicylic acid* every time he or she enters an aspirin prescription into a database. It's much easier for the doctor to teach the computer how to understand the spoken versions of these and similar medical phrases.

Expert Systems

Stated briefly, an expert system can solve problems that typically require expert knowledge. The opening scenario for this chapter describes such a system. In the SMART RESER-VATIONS system, expert system software is responsible for making decisions normally made by an airline scheduling and reservations executive. The logistics of an airline scheduling system can become complex. When normally scheduled flights are disrupted, chaos can result. It can be difficult, even for a human expert, to solve a scheduling crisis quickly enough to please customers. So, an expert system designed to provide rapid solutions to scheduling conflicts can be a power-ful aid for airline executives.

Like the human experts whose behavior they simulate, expert systems should be able to provide at least two basic services:

1. The system should be able to provide realistic solu-tions from relatively incomplete data.

2. The system should be able to explain how and why it arrived at a particular solution.

An expert system is able to make use of incomplete or po-tentially unreliable data by making logical assumptions. These assumptions are based upon the application of relevant rules and facts. Expert systems are usually created through the process of interviewing experts, gathering all of the im-portant information, and representing this information in the form of rules and facts. Although expert systems are one of the most popular and commercially successful applications of artificial intelligence, they do have their limitations. Their expertise is usually limited to a single area, thus they cannot solve problems outside of their domain of knowledge. Useful expert systems can however be created for a wide range of applications.

Many developers build generic expert system shells which can be used for different applications. An expert system shell contains all of the underlying logic and reasoning capabilities of the expert system. Once the necessary knowledge is added for a particular application, the program functions as a com-plete expert system.

The Turbo Prolog system is an excellent environment for developing and learning about expert systems. Its built-in features for creating rules and facts along with its powerful searching facilities can save a programmer many hours of time and frustration. In the chapters to follow, we will learn how to develop programming tools which will enable us to build expert systems for solving different types of problems.

Software Engineering

The biggest problem with computers is that they are too difficult to program. Millions of dollars are spent each year by large corporations to develop and maintain computer software. Fortunately, the techniques of developing and maintaining software have greatly improved over the years. Nevertheless, two very important problems facing the software developer still remain. Writing programs in such traditional third-generation languages as C, Pascal, or BASIC is too time consuming and most computer programs are too large and complex for people to fully understand and maintain.

The use of AI techniques in software development is a rapidly emerging trend. Software engineers are currently developing and working with a new generation of intelligent tools such as automated code generators, expert system debuggers, expert simulators, and tools for determining if a given program is running correctly. Many of these tools have the capability of performing tasks which could only be achieved, in the past, by experienced software engineers. With intelligent programming tools, more and more individuals will be able to develop their own custom software, thus making the computer a much more useful tool for society.

AI and Turbo Prolog

Now that we have discussed some of the applications of artificial intelligence, you might be wondering, Why is Turbo Prolog a good language for writing and exploring AI applications? Because AI programming requires a unique approach to problem solving, it makes sense for AI programmers to use a specialized programming language. Traditional third-generation languages, such as BASIC, COBOL, Pascal, and C tend to create more problems than solutions for AI programmers. Third-generation languages are procedural. That is, the programmer must plan for and code all the steps the computer will follow in solving a problem. Programming in a procedural language is machine oriented.

In Turbo Prolog, however, many procedural techniques are replaced by a declarative programming approach. The term *declarative* simply means that you can declare, or describe to the computer, the logical relationships which define the problem. For describing logical relationships, Turbo Prolog uses facts and rules. A *fact* is a statement expressing a relationship between one or more objects. If you create the statement:

```
John lives in Wyoming
```

you are expressing a fact. A *rule* on the other hand is a much more general statement about objects and their relationships. For example, the statement:

```
If someone lives in Wyoming than he/she might know
John
```

is a rule.

The facts and rules can be easily written in Turbo Prolog's simple syntax. Once these facts and rules are written, you request the program to solve the problem for you—a programmer's dream! Thus programming in Turbo Prolog consists of:

- Writing facts about objects and their relationships
- Creating rules about objects and their relationships
- Giving Turbo Prolog problems to solve

Advantages of Declarative Programming

Declarative languages like Turbo Prolog are ideal for writing AI programs because you can work at a very high level. Instead of thinking about the logic that the computer follows in solving a problem, you can concentrate on the actual problem relationships that can be used to create solutions. Also, by comparison with procedural languages, Turbo Prolog programs tend to be far more compact. A few pages of code written in a procedural language can often be reduced to a few lines in a declarative language.

However, don't be misled by the apparent simplicity of declarative programs. Writing a serious, practical AI program in a declarative language can often become complex. After all, in a true AI program, the objective is to simulate some aspect of intelligent human behavior. The job at hand might be to get the computer to learn from its previous activities, to make complex decisions, or to understand a story written in a natural language like English. To create these kinds of programs, it is important to spend time gathering all the knowledge the computer must have to solve problems presented by users. This knowledge base, in turn, must be represented to the computer in a usable form. Further, AI programs should be easy to modify. As programmers learn more about a given problem domain, they must be able to easily change programs to support different, more improved models.

Solving a Maze

The declarative approach to programming offers many benefits to the potential AI programmer. But to better understand the usefulness of the declarative approach, let's consider the task of searching through a small maze. Our maze shown in Figure 1.2 is not very complex; however, it should

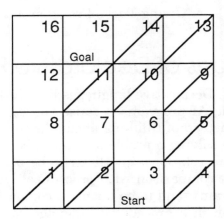

Figure 1.2   The Maze Problem

help to illustrate the differences between approaching a problem in a procedural language such as Turbo Pascal®and a declarative language like Turbo Prolog.

In the maze, each location which represents a possible move has a unique number in the upper right corner. The locations which are valid moves are shown as empty boxes and the paths or locations which are blocked are crossed out. Assuming our starting point is location 3 and our goal is location 15, then we can take the following path:

```
3 -> 6 -> 7 -> 8 -> 12 -> 16 -> 15.
```

To solve this maze in a procedural language, we would have to write instructions for all of the necessary steps. For example, we must write the instructions to determine if a move is a valid or invalid move and we must also write instructions to determine if we reach our goal location. To illustrate this procedural aspect, a sample program written in Turbo Pascal is shown in Listing 1.1.

Listing 1.1

```
PROGRAM MazeSearch;

{ This program is the Pascal version of the maze search. The program uses
  a procedural approach to solving the maze shown in Figure 1.2.
}

TYPE

  path_array = array[1..6, 1..2] OF Integer;

CONST

  max_path = 6;
  path    : path_array = ( (3,6), (6,7), (7,8), (8,12), (12,16), (16,15));


VAR

  goal, start : Integer;
```

(continued)

```
PROCEDURE Search(start, goal : Integer);

{ This procedure searches through the maze using recursion. }

VAR

 Found : Boolean;
 i     : Integer;

 BEGIN

  Found := FALSE;
  i := 0;
  REPEAT
    i := i + 1;
    IF start = path[i,1] THEN BEGIN
     Found := TRUE;
     Writeln('Move from ', path[i,1], ' To ', path[i,2]);
    END;
  UNTIL (Found) OR (i = max_path);

  IF Found THEN BEGIN
    IF path[i,2] <> Goal THEN
      Search(path[i,2], Goal)
    ELSE
      Writeln('Solution found.');
  END
  ELSE
    Writeln('No Solution for maze.');

END; {Procedure Search}

BEGIN    {Main program}
  Writeln('Enter start of maze');
  Readln(start);
  Writeln('Enter end of maze');
  Readln(goal);
  Search(start, goal);

END.
```

In this procedural approach, you must define both the data structures and the algorithms needed to solve the problem presented. With the maze problem, it is necessary to define a data structure to store the important information concerning which paths are available to travel. The chosen structure here is the array Path. This array is assigned the location indexes of valid moves. For example, the pair:

```
(3, 6)
```

indicates a valid move from location 3 to location 6 is available. Already you can see that this procedural implementation has disadvantages. If you were to increase or change the dimensions of the maze, you would have to change the data structure and rebuild the program.

When programming with a procedural language, you are also responsible for describing all of the necessary steps in order to solve the maze search. The instructions for this search are presented in the procedure Search. Search works by attempting to find a new location to move to. Of course the major disadvantage of our procedure Search is that it is written around the main data structure we are using to store the list of valid moves. Therefore, any change to our data structure must be followed up by a change in our search procedure in order for the maze program to run correctly.

The Turbo Prolog Approach

Now that a possible procedural solution in Turbo Pascal has been explored, let us turn to Turbo Prolog and the declarative method. The Turbo Prolog version is shown in Listing 1.2.

Listing 1.2

```
/* Turbo PROLOG version of maze search      */

predicates

    find_goal(integer, integer)
    path(integer, integer)

/* The predicate find_goal is the main clause which searches the maze */

/*  The predicate path is used to define the rules for moving through the
    maze
*/

clauses

    find_goal(Start, End):-

        path(Start, End), write("Goal is ", End), nl.
```

(continued)

```
find_goal(Start, End):-

        path(Start, G) , !,
        write("Move from ", Start, " To ", G), nl,
        find_goal(G, End).



/* Valid moves in the maze */

path(3, 6).
path(6, 7).
path(7, 8).
path(8, 12).
path(12, 16).
path(16, 15).
```

This version looks very simple by comparison because of Turbo Prolog's declarative nature. To begin with, you must define all of the facts which are part of the problem. These are represented by the clauses:

```
path(3, 6).
path(6, 7).
path(7, 8).

            etc.
```

These facts can be interpreted as stating:

```
There exists a path from 3 to 6.
There exists a path from 6 to 7.

            etc.
```

Because of this simple representation, changing the size or dimension of the maze would not affect our program very much. Only a potential change or addition of facts might be needed. The real power of Turbo Prolog lies in the fact that a program can be written so that the control flow is independent of the information the program needs. Needless to say, this feature will become extremely important to us as the more complex AI application programs are explored in later chapters.

The important thing to keep in mind is that you did not need to define the steps or algorithms for solving the maze in the Turbo Prolog version.

This task is performed by the clause:

```
find_goal(Start, End)
```

which serves as a rule for defining how the maze should be searched. This clause defines the important conditions:

```
If a valid move is available, then take it. If the
move takes us to the goal location then we are
done otherwise repeat the process.
```

This is all that is necessary to define a Turbo Prolog program to solve the maze problem. The final step that you must perform in order to run this program is to specify a goal. In this case the goal:

```
find_goal(3, 15)
```

is appropriate. Once you define this goal and represent it in Turbo Prolog, the system takes over and solves the problem for you. The capabilities for solving the problem are built into the Turbo Prolog system, thus making the programming task much easier.

To conclude this section on AI programming with Turbo programming, it seems appropriate to review the differences between the procedural approach to problem solving and the declarative approach. In the maze search problem, the program was written in a procedural language by following the steps:

- define the problem
- break the problem into small, unique tasks
- write algorithms or procedures to solve the defined tasks
- design data structures to represent the information needed to solve the problem

When the problem was solved using Turbo Prolog and its declarative style, the steps followed were:

- define the problem
- construct the rules and facts to represent the problem
- specify a goal to solve

As illustrated, Turbo Prolog offers you a different perspective to programming and problem solving. And since you are interested in learning about and developing AI applications, this new perspective can greatly enhance your programming and problem solving skills. Now that you have been introduced to the fascinating world of artificial intelligence and the uniqueness of Turbo Prolog for solving problems, you are ready to develop your skills of prolog programming for AI applications. In the chapters to follow, you will learn how Turbo Prolog can be used in many other ways to solve some of the unique problems related to artificial intelligence.

CHAPTER 2

Turbo Prolog Features

Learning to write artificial intelligence applications is more than just a matter of learning the general theories. To become proficient with AI programming, it is important to spend time mastering a programming language suited for AI applications. One of the best ways to gain a mastery over a programming language is to develop an understanding of how the language works and what it can do. The first chapter introduced some of the features of Turbo Prolog such as its declarative problem solving abilities. But Turbo Prolog has many other important features that must be understood before you can begin to write AI applications.

Besides providing a powerful built-in editor, compiler, and tracing facility, the Turbo Prolog system supports many advanced programming features. These features greatly simplify programming tasks such as searching for multiple solutions, pattern matching, and database programming. Of course, the more you understand how these features work, the easier it will be for you to create more complex programs.

This chapter presents the important features which will help you to develop a good working foundation for your AI programming explorations. To start out, let us take a tour through the underlying concepts behind the Turbo Prolog language to gain some understanding about how the language works.

How Turbo Prolog Works

When you attempt to solve a problem with Turbo Prolog, it is usually unnecessary to be concerned with the step by step details required to solve a particular problem. This, of course, is one of the major benefits of using a declarative language such as Turbo Prolog. However, as the complexity of your programs increase it becomes important that you develop an understanding about the basic fundamentals of how the Turbo Prolog system works. As an AI application becomes more complex, the number of comparison operations that must be performed by the computer rises exponentially. If the AI programmer is extravagant in the design, he or she will quickly be out of memory resources and/or have a very slow program.

The principles behind Turbo Prolog are not as complex as you might think. In fact, the Prolog language is actually based upon a single concept known as the resolution principle. This principle is responsible for setting the foundation for the current field of logic programming. It was developed in the 1960s by mathematicians and logicians who were experimenting with techniques for automatic theorem proving. Logic programming plays an important role in both AI applications and research. The notion that a computer can perform logically, which many people feel is the heart of intelligence, has intrigued computer scientists since the very beginnings of the digital computer.

The Resolution Principle

The resolution principle is simply a special type of inference rule. Rules of inference are very common and are used frequently whenever people make decisions about the world. In its simplest form, a rule of inference is a condition which is followed in order to transform a group of logical statements into a new group of statements. For example, if you create some statements about Turbo Prolog such as:

```
Turbo Prolog is a programming language.
Turbo Prolog is easy to learn.
Turbo Prolog works with symbolic language.
```

A rule of inference can be created to transform these statements into a new statement. Here is an inference rule you might make up:

```
If a programming language is easy to learn and the
language works with symbolic logic, then it is a
good programming language.
```

Applying this inference rule to the first group of statements enables you to create the new statement:

```
Turbo Prolog is a good programming language.
```

As shown, statements can be inferred from other statements by using a simple rule. Of course, rules of inference are natural to people, not computers. In order to use rules of inference in a programming language such as Prolog, a procedure must be followed to mechanize the process of making inferences. That's where the resolution principle comes in.

After being exposed to the concept of inference rules, you might be wondering "What exactly is the resolution principle?" The resolution principle is a single rule of inference which can be used to produce all of the possible conclusions that can be determined from a given set of facts or statements. It contains two parts: a definite clause and a negative clause. A definite clause is a statement such as:

```
John flys hot air balloons.
```

or written in Turbo Prolog:

```
flys(john, hot_air_balloons).
```

A negative clause is simply a statement which negates or makes the definite clause false. To turn the definite clause about John flying hot air balloons into a negative clause you could state:

```
It is not true that John flys hot air balloons.
```

or in Turbo Prolog:

```
not(flys(john, hot_air_balloons)).
```

Since the negative clause is easy to construct from a given definite clause, it is extremely well-suited for logic programming languages which must make automated inferences. In essence, this means that a computer program must be able to determine its own conclusions from a set of statements provided by a programmer. Needless to say, this principle is very important to many areas of theorem proving and artificial intelligence programming.

Now that the two important parts of the resolution principle have been presented, it is appropriate to look at an example which illustrates how the resolution principle is used. After a Turbo Prolog program is written and the necessary goals are specified for the computer to solve, the Turbo Prolog system must be able to decide if a solution can be found. For example, if you had two lists of numbers:

```
[1,2,3,5] and [4,6,9]
```

(lists are represented in Turbo Prolog with the syntax: '[ ]') and you wanted to append these two lists together to form a new list:

```
[1,2,3,5,4,6,9]
```

you must first write the program:

```
domains
  ilist = integers*
predicates
  append(ilist, ilist, ilist)
clauses
  append([], List, List).
  append([Head|Tail],List2,[Head|List3) :-
        append (Tail, List2, List3).
```

The clauses specified in this program are definite clauses which define the conditions under which the append operation is known to exist. The first clause states that if the empty list is appended with a second list, then the result is just the second list. The second clause states that the result of appending List2 with the list [Head|Tail] is the list [Head|List3]. This new list will then contain the same first element Head and the remainder List3, which is composed of Tail and List2. If you specify a goal for this program such as:

```
goal:
    append([1,2,3,5], [4,6,9], X).
```

The Turbo Prolog system would use the basic resolution principle to decide if this goal is valid or not. To perform this, the first step would be to create a negative clause out of the goal which would state:

```
There does not exist a list X such that X is the re-
sult of appending list [1,2,3,5] and list [4,6,9].
```

Of course, the clauses in the append program contradict this statement. Therefore, the task of the Prolog system is to show or prove this inconsistency. In the process of demonstrating this inconsistency, the inference technique will find the necessary counter examples to solve the goal. In this example, the list:

```
[1,2,3,5,4,6,9]
```

is created.

In the process of applying this simple resolution principle, Turbo Prolog uses a technique of substitution and matching called unification which is explored next.

Unification

Unification is a technique which defines the matching process used in Prolog programs to find solutions. The simplest demonstration of unification can be given with a short example. If you create a set of clauses in a program such as:

```
clauses
    builds(john, rockets).
    builds(mark, houses).
    builds(sue, computers).
```

and you specify the goal:

```
builds(sue, X).
```

The Turbo Prolog system will use unification to find a solution for the given goal. With your goal, you are actually asking Turbo Prolog the question:

```
What does Sue build?
```

To solve this goal, the set of defined clauses are searched by Turbo Prolog for a match. Of course, the answer in this case would be:

```
X = computers.
```

This matching process is called unification. Turbo Prolog attempts to match goals from left to right. This means that when you specify a goal, Turbo Prolog first looks at the leftmost part of the goal for a match with clauses stored in the database. In the case of the example goal:

```
builds(sue, X).
```

the leftmost part is the term sue. Turbo Prolog uses this term to find a match with one or more of the clauses defined in the program. If no match is found, the next term is used. Turbo Prolog repeats this procedure until all of the terms are examined or a match is found.

The unification process is a very powerful feature of Turbo Prolog. It provides automatic facilities for performing tasks such as general pattern-matching, assigning values to variables, and even testing for equalities and inequalities. For example, if you wanted to test a variable to see if it was assigned a given numeric value, you could specify a goal such as:

```
test(13).
```

Of course if you had an assertion in your clause database written as:

```
test(X):- X <> 12.
```

your goal would be true if X was not equal to 12. The unification process binds the variable X with the term "13" and therefore the expression:

```
13 <> 12
```

holds true.

This example illustrates the basic principles of the unification process. In a sense, unification can be compared to the operation of passing parameters to a procedure in a traditional language such as Pascal. In later chapters you will see how unification is used to construct more complex logical inferences for AI applications such as expert systems.

Backtracking

Turbo Prolog also contains an important built-in searching technique called backtracking which is useful for AI programming. Backtracking allows Turbo Prolog to work backward to try to find alternative solutions to a problem. When a goal is specified in Turbo Prolog, the system attempts to solve the sub-goals that are part of the goal. If a particular solution leads to a dead end, Turbo Prolog automatically backtracks and examines other sub-goals. This process continues until either a solution is found or all of the sub-goals lead to a dead end. To better understand how backtracking affects the outcome of a program, you should type in and try out the following example:

```
/*   The backtracking example */

predicates
        has_written(symbol, string)
        has_painted(symbol, string)
        is_classic(string)
        great_artist(symbol)

clauses
        has_written(j_d_salinger, "Catcher in the Rye").
        has_written(h_hesse, "Magister Ludi").
        has_written(h_hesse, "Siddhartha").
        has_written(papert, "Mindstorms").
        has_written(thoreau, "Walden").
        has_written(sheldrake, "A New Science of Life").
        has_written(wright, "The Natural House").


        has_painted(seurat, "Invitation To The Sideshow").
        has_painted(monet, "The Lilies").
        has_painted(van_gogh, "The Mulberry Tree").
        has_painted(picasso, "The Three Musicians").
        has_painted(barnes, "The People Eaters").
```

```
is_classic("Catcher in the Rye").
is_classic("Siddhartha").
is_classic("Walden").
is_classic("Invitation To The Side-show").
is_classic("The Lilies").
is_classic("The Mulberry Tree").
is_classic("The Three Musicians").

great_artist(Name):-
        has_written(Name, Work), is_classic (Work);
        has_painted(Name, Work), is_classic (Work);
```

After running this program and specifying the goal:

```
great_artist(h_hesse).
```

Turbo Prolog attempts to solve the simple rule:

```
great_artist(Name):-
        has_written(Name, Work), is_classic(Work);
        has_painted(Name, Work), is_classic(Work).
```

Of course, in order to solve this rule, the two sub-goals or facts "has_written" and "is_classic" must be proven. The first "has_written" sub-goal produces the result:

```
has_written(h_hesse, "Magister Ludi")
```

This is the first clause encountered in the program. Remember that the unification operation starts its search with the first defined clause, and then works its way through the other remaining clauses. When the next sub-goal is examined, "is_classic("Magister Ludi")," the operation fails because the example program does not contain an "is_classic" clause with the term "Magister Ludi." The failure of this sub-goal forces Turbo Prolog to backtrack and try an alternate solution. In this case, the backtracking starts with the "has_written" clause which now produces the result:

```
has_written(h_hesse, "Siddhartha")
```

After binding the term "Siddhartha" to the variable "Work," Turbo Prolog is now able to find a solution to the next sub-goal, "is_classic("Siddhartha")." Because this sub-goal succeeds, the main goal is now proven. The steps involved in solving our goal are shown in Figure 2.1.

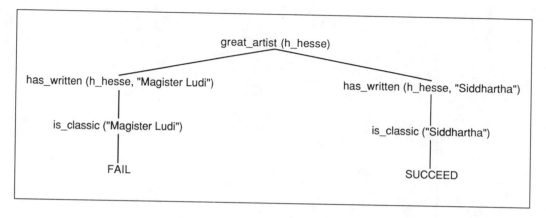

Figure 2.1   Representation of a Compound Object

Here the tree structure represents the hierarchical order of the sub-goal encountered in the solution.

As shown, Turbo Prolog backtracks whenever it cannot find a solution to a goal or sub-goal. Because most programs consist of complex goals—goals that are made up of numerous sub-goals—backtracking is a very important technique for controlling the flow of execution in programs. Backtracking can, however, become confusing in complex programs. Therefore it is important to understand where the backtracking points occur in a program. As an example, consider this complex goal:

```
goal:- Sg1, Sg2, Sg3.
```

Here the goal consists of three sub-goals: Sg1, Sg2, and Sg3. These sub-goals also consist of the sub-goals as shown:

```
Sg1:- Sga; Sgb.
Sg2:- Sgc.
Sg3:- Sgd, Sge.

Sge:- Sgf; Sgg.
```

Such complex goals can easily be represented in a tree structure called a goal tree. The goal tree is shown in Figure 2.2. Note that two of the sub-goals, Sg1 and Sge, can be satisfied by solving either of their sub-goals. The tree structure is a helpful device for representing goals and sub-goals because it

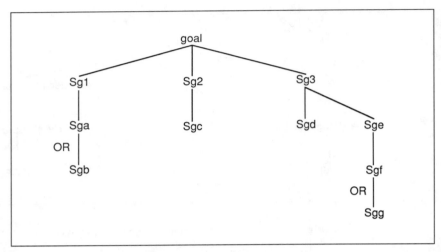

Figure 2.2   Representation of a Complex Goal

graphically indicates where the backtracking points can occur in a program. In the example, note that sub-goals Sg1, Sg2, and Sg3 must be proven in order to solve the main goal. As the goal tree indicates, these sub-goals can by proven by taking different paths. To illustrate how the backtracking works, let's look at two examples.

Assume that the sub-goal Sg1 is satisfied by solving Sga; Sg2 is satisfied by solving Sgc; and sub-goal Sg3 fails when it attempts to solve sub-goal Sgd. In this case, the system backtracks to sub-goal Sg1 because this sub-goal has two options: Sga and Sgb. The backtracking starts with the first sub-goal that contains an alternate solution. At this backtracking point, the system now attempts to solve sub-goal Sgb and if this sub-goal succeeds, the system will attempt to solve sub-goals Sg2 and Sg3 again.

In the second case, assume that again Sg1 is satisfied by solving Sga; Sg2 is satisfied by solving Sgc; and this time Sg3 satisfies sub-goal Sgd. However, in order to succeed, sub-goal Sg3 must also solve sub-goal Sge. Now, if sub-goal Sge attempts to solve sub-goal Sgf and fails, the backtracking occurs at Sge because this sub-goal contains an alternate: sub-goal Sgg.

When working with complex goals, the important issue to keep in mind is that backtracking occurs with the first available sub-goal.

Non-Deterministic Programming

Before ending the tour of the concepts underlying the Turbo Prolog language, we need to introduce the important concept of non-deterministic programming. Most of the problems people face in their day to day lives often have more than one solution. However, most computer programs written in traditional languages have no capabilities for handling multiple solutions. If you want to write computer programs which are capable of simulating intelligent thought, then you must think about developing techniques for creating programs which can handle multiple solutions. Fortunately, logic programming languages, such as Turbo Prolog, support what is called non-deterministic programming—the ability of a computer program to find more than one solution to a given problem on its own. Non-determinism is a concept which does not seem very natural to most procedural programmers. However, once you understand the basic principle and how it can be used, you will find that it is very useful for creating powerful programs.

Traditional programming languages such as BASIC or Pascal are considered to be deterministic. Once a program is created in one of these languages, the computer will only find the solutions you instruct it to look for. The outcome is essentially determined by the programmer who wrote the instructions. With Turbo Prolog, a non-deterministic language, the computer in a sense has the ability to search for its own solutions without the programmer giving explicit instructions. Of course, Turbo Prolog does not have a mind of its own and thus it can only simulate non-deterministic behavior with its backtracking and searching facilities. These capabilities provide Turbo Prolog with a feature that makes it well suited for specialized AI applications such as expert systems or natural language query systems. In such systems, it is important for the application to provide the user with more than one solution if one is available. Of course, the technique of non-determinism can be simulated in such traditional procedural languages as C or Pascal, however, it is the programmer's responsibility to make certain the program operates in a non-deterministic way.

To better understand how non-deterministic programming is supported in Turbo Prolog, let's look at a few examples. The first example presents a simple program with the set of clauses as shown:

```
predicates
  makes(symbol, symbol)
  operates(symbol, symbol)

clauses
  makes(tom, money).
  makes(sharon, friends).
  makes(steve, friends).
  operates(harold, radios).
  operates(harold, computers).
  operates(sharon, printer).
```

If a goal is specified, such as:

```
goal: makes(Who, friends).
```

the Turbo Prolog system responds:

```
Who = sharon
Who = steve
```

Thus, in response to the question: Who makes friends?, Turbo Prolog uses a sequential search technique to search through the database of clauses provided. The search algorithm is comprehensive. Turbo Prolog examines each clause for a potential match. If more than one solution is present, Turbo Prolog will find them all.

If you want to limit the search so that Turbo Prolog will only find one solution, you can use the cut operator, '!'. If you provide the goal:

```
goal: operates(harold, X), !.
```

Turbo Prolog responds with the solution:

```
X = radios.
```

If you did not use the cut operator, Turbo Prolog would have displayed:

```
X = radios
X = computers
```

When the cut operator is present, Turbo Prolog searches the stored facts until the first solution is found. But after finding one solution, Turbo Prolog will not continue searching for other solutions. With the cut operator, you can keep Turbo Prolog from operating in a non-deterministic manner. The cut operator keeps Turbo Prolog from backtracking past the point from which the cut operator is placed.

The second example illustrates how Turbo Prolog uses backtracking to support the non-deterministic programming concept. Here is the program:

```
predicates

    reads(symbol, symbol)
    writes(symbol, symbol)
    is_smart(symbol)

clauses
    reads(karen, novels).
    reads(john, newspapers).
    reads(kathy, magazines).
    reads(oscar, novels).

    writes(kelly, letters).
    writes(oscar, novels).
    writes(john, articles).

    is_smart(Person):-
    reads(Person, novels),
    writes(Person, novels).
```

If you specify the goal:

```
goal: is_smart(Who).
```

which is a request to the Turbo Prolog system to determine the answer to the question: Who is smart? Turbo Prolog will use backtracking to solve the goal. When the clause:

```
is_smart
```

is processed, Turbo Prolog looks for a match between the clause:

```
reads(Person, novels)
```

and one of the other clauses defined in the program. A match is found with the clause:

```
reads(karen, novels).
```

At this point, the variable Person is bound to the term karen. This program next tries to find a match for:

```
writes(karen, novels).
```

Of course, there is no match for this clause. Because of this, Turbo Prolog must backtrack (work backward) and attempt to solve the original goal.

Thinking About Facts and Rules

By now, you should have a basic understanding about resolution, unification, and non-determinism—the principles behind Turbo Prolog. And now that these important concepts have been discussed, it is time to move on and examine some of the powerful features of Turbo Prolog that will be used in later chapters to build AI applications. The two essential components used in all of the Turbo Prolog programs you will develop are facts and rules. Taken together, these two components are responsible for defining the logic or flow of control in a Turbo Prolog program.

Facts

The building blocks of Turbo Prolog programs for AI applications are simply facts. Facts are used in programs to describe the relationships between objects. For example, if you wanted to state a fact about zebras, you could write:

```
have(zebras, black_stripes).
```

This simple fact says that zebras have black stripes. You could also think of this as stating that there is a relationship between zebras and black stripes—the relationship "have." Facts are easy to write in Turbo Prolog. Every fact contains a relationship and one or more arguments. The relationship is always written first and the arguments are listed inside the parentheses.

When you are writing programs which use AI techniques, such as expert systems or natural language interfaces, one of the first things you must do is gather up all of the important facts. In order to be useful, these facts must relate to the problem you are trying to solve. Once all of the necessary facts are collected, it is a relatively simple matter to represent them in Turbo Prolog. The collection of facts along with the relevant rules serve as the foundation of what is commonly called the knowledge base. Knowledge bases are used in AI programs to store the expertise of human experts. In later chapters you will learn how to create and manipulate knowledge bases for AI applications such as expert systems.

The Turbo Prolog system is a good environment for creating and modifying knowledge bases because facts can easily be added to a working program and tested. But keep in mind that facts not only serve as definitions of relations between objects, but also as descriptions of situations. For example, if you wanted to describe the following situation:

```
Yesterday I saw a man who was dressed in a large
overcoat walk into the drugstore. Shortly thereaf-
ter, I heard a shot and then I saw the man running
from the store with a pistol in his hand.
```

In Turbo Prolog, you could represent this situation with the following set of facts:

```
day(yesterday).
saw(i, man).
dressed(man, in_large_overcoat).
walk_into(man, drug_store).
heard(i, shot).
saw(i, man_running).
held(man, pistol).
```

This representation does not contain all of the exact details found in the descriptive sentences. However, it should illustrate the power of Turbo Prolog in its ability to describe situations with the use of facts.

Building Complex Facts

Turbo Prolog allows you to combine objects and relationships together to create complex facts. For example, if you had the following facts in your database:

```
writes(dan, prolog_books).
book_type("AI Programming", prolog).
author_of(dan, "AI Programming").
```

You could easily combine these facts to create the compound fact:

```
writes(dan, book_type("AI Programming", prolog)).
```

In this case the predicate "writes" is called a compound object. This object consists of two parts: the term "dan" and the predicate "book_type." Book_type functions as an argument for the main predicate "writes." The technical term for this argument is a *functor*. The functor itself has arguments which are called components. The formal syntax for compound objects can be written as:

```
compound_object(object, functor(component, component)).
```

The structure of the "writes" compound object can be represented as shown in Figure 2.3.

Compound objects are unique data structures and they must be explicitly declared in Turbo Prolog. The declaration for these data structures must be placed in the domain section of a program. As an example, here is one possible declaration of the compound object presented in the previous example:

```
domains
    category = symbol
    author = symbol
    title = string
    type = style(category); book_type(title, category)
```

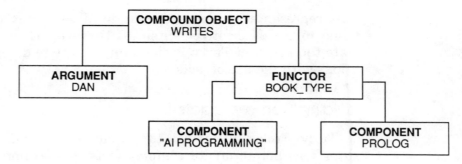

Figure 2.3 Representation of a Compound Object

```
predicates
    writes(author, type)
```

Note that the domain "type" is defined as a functor. The semi-colon acts as an OR operator and lets you define domains that can have multiple interpretations. In this case, you can write clauses that look like:

```
writes(jim, style(fiction))
```

or clauses like:

```
writes(jim, book_type("A Trip to the Moon", fiction)).
```

The advantage with such a declaration is you can easily create facts that are flexible.

Using Complex Facts

Complex facts can be very important to AI applications such as expert systems where the knowledge is often stored in a hierarchical order. Knowledge that is naturally represented in a tree-type structure can easily be coded in Turbo Prolog using compound objects. As an example, assume you have the set of relationships shown in Figure 2.4.

These relationships could be described with the following declarations:

```
domains
    computer  = computer(monitor, keyboard, main_unit)
    monitor   = monitor(tube, display)
    keyboard  = keyboard(keys, case)
    keys      = keys (space_bar, function_keys,
                    other_keys)
    main_unit = main_unit (power_supply, processor_board,
                    memory, disk_drive)
```

The main advantage of using complex facts is that they allow you to group related information together in a very concise manner. This can be a real asset for complex programs which are composed of many facts. In later chapters, you will learn how to apply the techniques of using complex facts to develop applications such as natural language processing programs and expert systems.

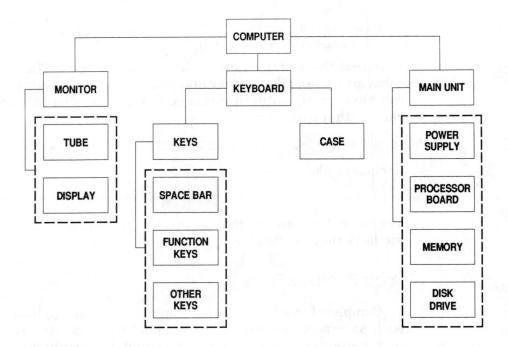

Figure 2.4   Representation of Computer Relationships

Rules

Rules allow you to create general statements. They are used to define new relationships based on facts already known. Rules can be constructed by grouping related or unrelated facts together. For example, if the following relationships are defined:

```
knows(tom, french).
knows(pete, spanish).
knows(laurie, latin).
studies(tom, prolog).
studies(laurie, pascal).
```

You can construct the following rule:

```
is_smart(Person):-
  knows(Person, french),
  studies(Person, prolog).
```

The facts "knows" and "studies" are unrelated; however, you can group them together as shown to form the rule which states:

```
A person is smart if he/she knows French and stud-
ies Prolog.
```

Rules are extremely important in Prolog programs since they actually define the manner in which the facts in a program are interpreted. Rules and facts are used in Turbo Prolog programs to create knowledge bases. In later chapters you will learn how to use rules to construct expert systems.

Rules are very simple to construct. They always consist of two distinct parts: a head and a body:

```
head ( )  :-
  body.
```

The head serves as the name or premise of the rule. The ":-" symbol functions as the word *if*; in fact the keyword "if" can be used in Turbo Prolog as a replacement for the ":-" symbol. The body of a rule consists of the set of sub-goals or facts that must be true in order for the rule to be valid. In this respect, the rule:

```
hungry(Person)  :-
  not(eat(Person, lunch)).
```

states that a person is hungry if he/she did not eat lunch.

Although rules cannot be nested in Turbo Prolog, they can be combined to create such complex structures as if-then-else statements. For example, if you wanted to create the following rule structure:

```
If the car starts
and there is no traffic
then the driver will get to work on time
Else the driver will be late
```

you could write these rules as:

```
work(Driver, on_time):-
  starts(Driver, car),
  traffic(Driver, false).
work(Driver, late).
```

Note that this code contains two clauses. The first clause, "work," represents the "if" part of the if-then-else rule and the second clause represents the "else" part. If you test this rule by specifying a goal such as:

```
goal:
 work(fred, X).
```

Turbo Prolog will test the first "work" clause found in the database and if that clause fails, it will test the next one. In this respect, the clauses function as an if-then-else rule. When writing these types of rules, it is important to place them in the right order. For example, if you listed the "else" part of the above rule first:

```
work(Driver, late).
```

you would completely change the meaning of the rule.

Working with Domains

Facts and rules are not the only structures used in Turbo Prolog programs. Programs must also contain data structures. In Turbo Prolog, data structures are called domains. And one of Turbo Prolog's strong points is that it supports a full set of domain types from which you can build more complex and useful structures. The basic domains provided by the system include:

```
integer
real
character
string
symbol
file
```

The integer and real domains are useful for programs which work with numerical calculations. Programs which perform symbolic processing on the other hand, use the character, string, and symbol domains. In the AI programming applications presented in later chapters, the domains used for symbolic processing will be used extensively. With these basic domains you can create lists which serve as important structures for the AI programs and tools you will create in later chapters. In order to develop a better understanding about the manner in which lists are created and used in Turbo Prolog, they will be discussed next.

Lists in Turbo Prolog

The list is a very useful and important data structure for AI programming applications. In fact one very popular AI programming language, LISP, is designed completely around the list structure. A list in Turbo Prolog is a sequence of elements presented in a specific order. Each element in a list is called a member. For example:

```
[mary, mike, john, yolanda]
```

is a list with members: mary, mike, john, yolanda. Of course, if the list were written as:

```
[mike, john, yolanda, mary]
```

it would be a different list because of the change in the order of its members. Lists are represented in Turbo Prolog with the use of the square brackets. The simplest list you can write is the empty list which is represented as:

```
[ ]
```

Here is a list of vowels represented as symbols:

```
[a, e, i, o, u]
```

And here is a list of names represented as strings:

```
["Hal", "Steve", "Gina"]
```

As shown, you can create lists of different domain types. For example, if you wanted to create a list of symbols you would declare the list as:

```
domains
    symlist = symbol*
```

The asterisk indicates that the domain you are creating, symlist, is a list structure of type symbol. Once this domain is declared, you can define predicates and clauses which can be used to operate on lists of symbols. In the next chapter, you

will learn how to write programs that work with lists as you
start building your AI tools.

Strings

The string domain type is another structure which is important for writing AI applications. You can actually view a
string as a list of characters. For example, the string:

```
"This is a string"
```

can be represented as:

```
['T','h','i','s','','i','s','','a','','s','t','r','i','n','g']
```

Of course, in most instances it is easier to work with strings
than lists of characters. In fact Turbo Prolog provides some
built-in predicates which make string manipulation much
easier.

The maximum number of characters which can be bound
to a string variable in Turbo Prolog is 64K. A string constant
on the other hand, can only consist of a maximum of 250 characters. The string domain is very useful for representing
words and sentences. Because of this, it is an ideal structure
for natural language processing applications.

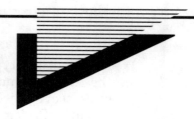

CHAPTER 3

Building Your AI Toolbox

To reduce the complexity of writing AI programs, you will find it helpful to create your own toolbox of common Turbo Prolog predicates. Many applications require such tasks as string and list processing, control strategies, pattern matching, search strategies, and database manipulation. If you take the time to develop a set of useful tools to perform such functions, you can develop applications quicker and easier. Of course, one advantage of a well written tool is that you can use it for many applications. Thus you are eliminating the need to reinvent the wheel each time you develop a new program. Also, the tool approach to programming provides you with a good methodology for learning how to get the most out of a programming language.

In this chapter you will learn how to design and code some of the important programming tools that should be a part of your personal toolbox for developing AI applications. In later chapters you will be able to use some of these tools. This modular approach will quickly help you to get started thinking about the types of programming problems which confront the AI programmer. The first section of this chapter presents some tools which are useful for developing control strategies in Turbo Prolog. In following sections, you will also learn how to develop tools for string and list processing.

Selecting and Building the Right Tool

Just as a carpenter is careful to select the right tool for building a house—he wouldn't use a saw to nail two pieces of wood together—you should also be methodical about the tools you develop and use for your programming applications. If the tools you construct are general enough, you will find that they can be used in many different applications. Often the need for a specific tool arises when you are in the middle of writing a program. In such cases the important design issue to consider is: can the tool be written in such a way that it will be useful for other applications? Also, many useful tools can be created by using other tools as a foundation. In this respect you can create complex programs by piecing together simple tools. For example, you could build a program for pattern matching by using string handling tools as your foundation.

Control Strategies

Turbo Prolog provides some built-in control strategies such as backtracking; however, other powerful techniques can be developed easily. The first control strategy technique that you should include in your toolbox is the concept of looping, or iteration. Most procedural languages such as C, Pascal, and BASIC provide built-in statements for creating loops. In Turbo Prolog, one of the easiest loops to write is the infinite loop, which is called the repeat-fail loop.

The Repeat-Fail

The basic repeat-fail loop is written using a recursive definition consisting of two parts:

```
repeat.
repeat :- repeat.
```

The first predicate acts as the termination part and the second predicate consists of a simple recursive operation. This repeat predicate is very powerful and you can use it whenever you need a section of your code to execute repetitively. For example, if you wanted to print a continual message on the screen you could write:

```
print :-
     repeat, write("Infinite Loop"), nl, fail.
```

The print predicate calls the repeat predicate which will always succeed. The first time repeat is called, only the simple clause "repeat." is accessed. Because this predicate succeeds, the other predicates—write, nl, and fail—are executed. Fail causes the print clause to fail; therefore, the print predicate will backtrack and call the clause or rule:

```
repeat :- repeat.
```

This action starts the infinite loop. The repeat clause sets a backtracking point and when the fail predicate is encountered, the backtracking is started which creates the looping control. As you can see, the repeat-fail loop is created by using the following sequence of calls:

```
Loop
----
     repeat,
     .
     .
     .
     fail.
```

The repeat-fail loop can be used for many practical applications, especially for tasks related to data input. Often it is necessary to check the responses typed in by the user of a program and if the information is incorrect, the program should ask the user to type in the information again. For example, assume you wanted to write a program to provide information about customers stored in a knowledge base. The first step would be to write a predicate to test the user's input with the information stored. The following predicate check_name performs this function using the repeat/fail combination:

```
/* The repeat/fail combination */

predicates

    repeat
    check_name
    match(symbol)

clauses

    repeat.
    repeat :- repeat.

    check_name :-
        repeat,
        write("Enter Name"), nl,
        readln(Name),
        match(Name),!.

    match(tom).
    match(carol).
    match(cynthia).
    match(teri).
```

Note that the fail predicate is missing from this code. This
function is implied by the match predicate. If you run this
program by typing in the goal, check_name, and you enter a
name that is not represented with one of the match predicates, match will fail and force the repeat loop to execute. The
loop will continue until a correct name is entered. In this
sense, the repeat loop functions as a conditional loop.

The repeat predicate is implemented as a recursive function. Note that this predicate makes calls to itself to achieve
its iteration. Recursive programming is one of the fundamental principles of programming in Turbo Prolog; therefore, it is
important to develop some tools for using this control strategy
effectively.

Stepping into Recursion

Recursion is a very powerful control strategy that can easily be implemented for solving both numeric and symbolic
problems. The fundamental principle of recursion consists of
defining a relationship or process in terms of itself. For example, you could define a tree as consisting of branches which

contain branches, which contain branches, etc. This technique of using recursion to define something that has not yet been completely defined might seem unnatural to you; however, without recursion it would not be possible to solve complex problems in Turbo Prolog.

Here is an example to help you understand recursion. Suppose you had a building that had six floors. You could make the statement that two floors are a part of your building if they are neighbors (one on top of the other—see Figure 3.1). This rule can be written:

```
part_of(F1, F2):-
    neighbor(F1, F2).
```

which states that:

```
For any two floors, F1 and F2,
    F1 and F2 are part of a building if F1 and F2
    are neighbors.
```

This rule is very simple; however, it does not tell you anything about the floors which are not direct neighbors. You could, however, indirectly include all of the floors by using recursion to create another definition such as:

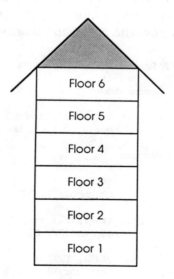

Figure 3.1   A Simple Building

```
part_of(F1, F2) :-
    neighbor(F1, X),
    part_of(X, F2).
```

which now states:

```
For any two floors, F1 and F2,
   F1 and F2 are part of the building if
   there exists another floor X such that
   X is a neighbor of F1
   and X and F2 are part of the building.
```

Note that the predicate part_of is used in its own definition. This definition might seem confusing because it is recursive: it defines itself by using its own definition! Actually, the recursion serves as a natural technique for explaining these relationships. Figure 3.2 illustrates how the recursive definition is defined. Note that the two floors, floor 6 and floor 1, are related in the sense that they each have floors that are neighbors. If you examine the diagram, you will see that floor 6 is connected with floor 1 because floor 6 has a neighbor, floor 5, which has a neighbor, floor 4, and so on.

The complete program for solving this problem is shown next. You should type it in at this point and try out some examples with the predicate, part_of. You might find it helpful to use the trace mode built into Turbo Prolog to better understand how the recursion works:

```
/* A Recursive Definition */

    predicates

        part_of(symbol, symbol)
        neighbor(symbol, symbol)

    clauses

        part_of(F1, F2) :-
            neighbor(F1, F2).

        part_of(F1, F2) :-
            neighbor(F2, F1).

        part_of(F1, F2) :-
            neighbor(F1, X),
            part_of(X, F2).
```

```
part_of(F1, F2) :-
     neighbor(F2, X),
     part_of(X, F1).
```
or neighbour (x, F1),
    part-of (F2,x).

```
neighbor(floor1, floor2).
neighbor(floor2, floor3).
neighbor(floor3, floor4).
neighbor(floor4, floor5).
neighbor(floor5, floor6).
```

With the trace mode on, you can specify a goal such as:

```
part_of(floor1, floor6).
```

and watch the recursion. Note that two predicates have been added:

```
part_of(F1, F2) :-
     neighbor(F2, F1).

part_of(F1, F2) :-
     neighbor(F2, X),
     part_of(X, F1).
```

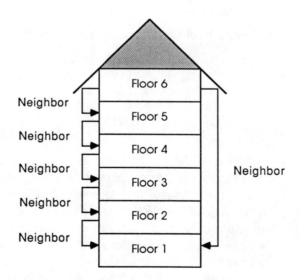

Figure 3.2   Recursive Relationship Between Floor 1 and Floor 6

These predicates allow goals such as:

```
part_of(floor6. floor1) .-
```

to be tested. Here, the order of the arguments is reversed; however, the part_of predicate will still find an answer because it contains predicates which will reverse the order of the arguments to fit the structure of the stored facts. Remember that the facts are stored in the form:

```
neighbor(floor1, floor2)
```

and therefore only express one-way relationships. In such a case, often it is easier to add additional predicates rather than add more facts. This is a useful programming technique when working with programs that contain large databases.

Controlling the Loop

Recursion can also be used to create conditional control structures such as a While-Loop. This type of loop is very popular in procedural languages such as Pascal. It is structured as:

```
While <condition> Do
   statement;
```

In Turbo Prolog, you can write such a loop as:

```
loop(Count, Limit) :-
    Count < Limit,
    write(Count),
    Nc = Count + 1,
    loop(Nc, Limit).

loop(_,_).
```

The main loop clause performs the operation of testing to see if the Count variable has exceeded the limit specified by the Limit argument. When it does, this clause fails and the second clause loop(_,_), is called. Since this clause always succeeds, a solution can always be found. You could easily modify this predicate to work with either logical or numerical expressions by changing the head of the clause, loop(Count,Limit) :-, and the first statement in the clause.

Characters and Strings

Turbo Prolog provides some built-in predicates, such as str_char, str_len, frontchar, frontstr, fronttoken, and concat to handle strings and characters. These predicates are useful for many applications; however, you may need more specialized tools for performing such tasks as pattern recognition or natural language processing. In this section, you will learn how to develop some useful character and string handling tools.

Character handling tools are easy to write in Turbo Prolog. For example, if you want to write a predicate to determine if a character is an ASCII digit you could write the clause:

```
isdigit(Ch) :-
    Ch >= '0', Ch <= '9'.
```

Isdigit tests the argument, Ch, to see if it is in the range of ASCII 0 to 9. Another simple tool could be written to test a character to see if it is a letter of the alphabet:

```
isalpha(Ch) :-
    Ch >= 'A', Ch <= 'Z'.

isalpha(Ch) :-
    Ch >= 'a', Ch <= 'z'.
```

Note that this predicate consists of two parts. The first tests the character to see if it is an uppercase letter and the second tests for a lowercase letter. If you wanted to extend the last two tools and create a more general tool to test a character to see if it is an alphanumeric character, you could write:

```
isalnum(Ch) :-
    isalpha(Ch), ! ; isdigit(Ch).
```

This predicate uses Turbo Prolog's OR operator, ";", to call either the isalpha predicate or the isdigit. The advantage of using tools in this manner is that you can create more complex functions by putting together simple tools.

The previous character tools are useful for comparing characters; however, other tools are necessary if you want to perform functions such as modifying characters. For example, assume you are writing a pattern matching program and you need to convert uppercase letters to lowercase. You could start with the simple predicates:

```
predicates:

islower(Ch) :-
    Ch >= 'a', Ch <= 'z'.

isupper(Ch) :-
    Ch >= 'A', Ch <= 'Z'.
```

you could write a conversion tool:

```
tolower(Sch, Tch):-
    isupper(Sch),
    char_int(Sch, Val),
    Cv = Val + $20,
    char_int(Tch, Cv).

tolower(Sch, Tch):-
    islower(Sch), Tch = Sch.
```

to perform this task. Note that the tolower predicate consists of two parts. The first converts a lowercase letter by increasing its ASCII value by 20 hex. The second part tests to see if the character is already a lowercase letter and if this is true it returns the character. This is important because it guarantees that the conversion tool will work for all cases. In this example, the tool converts an uppercase letter to its lowercase equivalent. It fails if the specified character is not a letter; thus, your calling program will know if the specified character was valid.

Although these character tools are simple, they are useful for many practical applications. To help you build a more complete library of such tools, a set of character predicates is provided next. You should type these in and save them in an include file so that they can be used by other programs. Here is the complete set:

chartool.pro

```
/* The Complete Set of Character Handling Tools */

predicates

    isalnum(char)      /* Test for alphanumeric (A--Z, a--z, or 0--9) */
    isalpha(char)      /* Test for a letter in (A--Z or a--z) */
```

```
isascii(char)       /* Test for character in ASCII set (0--7Fh)  */
iscntrl(char)       /* Test for a control character (0--1Fh or 7Fh) */
isdigit(char)       /* Test for a digit (0--9)  */
isgraph(char)       /* Test for printable characters expect space */
                    /* range of printable characters (21h--7Eh) */
islower(char)       /* Test for lower case letter (a--z)        */
isprint(char)       /* Test for printable character (20h--7Eh)  */
ispunct(char)       /* Test for a punctuation character */
isspace(char)       /* Test for a whitespace character  */
isupper(char)       /* Test for upper case letter (A--Z)    */
isxdigit(char)      /* Test for a Hex digit (A--F, a--f, or 0--9) */


tolower(char, char)        /* Convert character to lower case  */
toupper(char, char)        /* Convert character to upper case  */
toxdigit(integer, char)    /* convert integer 0 -16 to hex digit */
```

clauses

```
isalnum(Ch) :-
    isalpha(Ch), ! ; isdigit(Ch).

isalpha(Ch) :-
    Ch >= 'A', Ch <= 'Z'.

isalpha(Ch) :-
    Ch >= 'a', Ch <= 'z'.

isascii(Ch) :-
    char_int(Ch, Val),
    Val >= 0, Val <= $7f.

iscntrl(Ch) :-
    char_int(Ch, Val),
    Val >= 0, Val <= $1f.

iscntrl(Ch) :-
    char_int(Ch, Val),
    Val = $7f.

isdigit(Ch) :-
    Ch >= '0', Ch <= '9'.

isgraph(Ch) :-
    char_int(Ch, Val),
    Val >= $21, Val <= $7e.
```

(continued)

```
islower(Ch):-
    Ch >= 'a', Ch <= 'z'.

isprint(Ch):-
    char_int(Ch, Val),
    Val >= $20, Val <= $7f.

ispunct(Ch):-
    not(iscntrl(Ch)), not(isalnum(Ch)).

isspace(Ch):-
    Ch = ' ';
    char_int(Ch, Val),
    Val = $09.

isspace(Ch):-
    char_int(Ch, Val),
    Val = $0d.

isupper(Ch):-
    Ch >= 'A', Ch <= 'Z'.

isxdigit(Ch):-
    isdigit(Ch); Ch >= 'A', Ch <= 'F'; Ch >= 'a', Ch <= 'f'.

toupper(Sch, Tch):-
    islower(Sch),
    char_int(Sch, Val),
    Cv = Val - $20,
    char_int(Tch, Cv).

toupper(Sch, Tch):-
    isupper(Sch), Tch = Sch.

tolower(Sch, Tch):-
    isupper(Sch),
    char_int(Sch, Val),
    Cv = Val + $20,
    char_int(Tch, Cv).

tolower(Sch, Tch):-
    islower(Sch), Tch = Sch.

toxdigit(Val, Ch):-
    Val >= 0, Val <= 9,
    Cv = Val + $30,                 /* ascii code for '0' */
    char_int(Ch, Cv).

toxdigit(Val, Ch):-
    Val > 9, Val <= 15,
    Cv = Val + $37,                 /* ascii code for 'A' - 10 */
    char_int(Ch, Cv).
```

Working with Strings

Strings are the second important data type in Turbo Prolog. Fortunately, a few basic string handling tools are provided with Turbo Prolog. However, you will need other tools for writing complex and useful programs. In this section, some useful string tools are developed to help you get started in creating a more complete library of string tools. The tools developed in this section are used to perform operations such as searching for characters and sub-strings in strings, inserting characters and sub-strings, deleting characters and sub-strings, and replacing characters and sub-strings. The first tool presented, strcfind, is used for searching for a character in a string. Here is the tool:

```
/* The Strcfind Tool */

predicates

    strcfind(string, char, integer)     /* Search for a char in string */
    findc(string, char, integer, integer)

clauses

    strcfind(Srcstr, Ch, Pos):-
        str_len(Srcstr, Size),              /* get string length */
        findc(Srcstr, Ch, Pos, Size), ! .

    findc(Str, _, _, _):-
        str_len(Str, 0), fail.      /* if length =0, return false */

    findc(Str, Ch, Pos, Size):-
        frontchar(Str, Fc, Rest),
        Ch = Fc,                        /* found matching character */
        str_len(Rest, Subl),            /* get substring length     */
        Pos = Size - Subl.              /* determine character pos  */

    findc(Str, Ch, Pos, Size):-
        frontchar(Str, _, Rest),        /* remove first character   */
        findc(Rest, Ch, Pos, Size).
```

Strcfind uses three arguments: Srcstr, Ch, and Pos. The first argument contains the string to be searched and the second argument holds the specified character for the search. Finally, the third argument contains the position of the character in the string, if a match is found. Strcfind performs two basic tasks: it determines the length of the given string and it calls findc, which is the predicate responsible for searching for an occurrence of the character in the string. The string's length is determined by calling the built-in predicate str_len.

Findc is implemented as a recursive predicate. The first condition it tests for is the case where the given string is the null string (no characters). If this situation occurs, findc fails and the calling predicate, strcfind, also fails. The main part of findc consists of the code:

```
findc(Str, Ch, Pos, Size):-
    frontchar(Str, Fc, Rest),
    Ch = Fc,
    str_len(Rest, Subl),
    Pos = Size - Subl.
```

Note that the built-in predicate frontchar is used. This predicate performs the task of extracting the first character from the string. If the extracted character is equal to the character specified for the search, then findc succeeds and the position of this character is returned. Whenever this predicate fails, the final findc predicate is called. This predicate is responsible for reducing the string by one character and calling itself with the new string. As an example, if you call strcfind with the following values:

```
strcfind("Hello", 'l', Pos).
```

findc processes the string in the following steps:

```
"Hello"
"ello"
"llo"
```

At this point, findc succeeds and returns a value of 3 for the string position. Note that the search (recursion) stops as soon as findc finds the first occurrence of the specified character. Of course, you could also develop a tool to search for the last occurrence of a character in a string. As a hint, one approach would be to first reverse the order of the characters in the string.

The capability of the strcfind predicate can be extended by rewriting the tool so that it searches for sub-strings instead of a single character. In this case, the tool would be able to find sub-strings such as "ball" in a string like "baseball" or "racquetball." Here is the new tool:

```
/* The Strsfind Tool */

predicates

    strsfind(string, string, integer)      /* Search for first substring
                                               in string */
    matchs(string, string, integer, integer)

clauses

    strsfind(Srcstr, Substr, Pos):-
        str_len(Srcstr, Size),                /* get length of string  */
        str_len(Substr, Ssize),               /* get length of substring */
        matchs(Srcstr, Substr, Ssize, Sub1), !, /* check for match */
        Pos = Size - (Ssize + Sub1) + 1.       /* update position  */

    matchs(Str1, _, _, _):-                    /* fail on null string */
        Str1 = "", fail.

    matchs(Str1, Str2, Size, Sub1):-
        frontstr(Size, Str1, First, Rest),     /* extract substring  */
        First = Str2,                          /* substring matches  */
        str_len(Rest, Sub1).                   /* get length of rest of

    matchs(Str1, Str2, Size, Sub1):-
        frontchar(Str1, _, Rest),
        matchs(Rest, Str2, Size, Sub1).
```

Note that this predicate, strsfind, is constructed like the previous tool. Again, three parameters are used. In this case, however, the second parameter contains the sub-string used for the search. The search occurs in the clause, matchs, as shown:

```
matchs(Str1, Str2, Size, Sub1):-
    frontstr(Size, Str1, First, Rest),
    First = Str2,
    Str_len(Rest, Sub1).
```

Here, frontstr, the built-in predicate, extracts the first group of characters equal to the size of the specified sub-string from the source string. This new string, stored in the argument First, is compared with the sub-string and if a match occurs this predicate succeeds. If the strings do not match, control falls down to the last matchs clause which is:

```
matchs(Str1, Str2, Size, Sub1):-
    frontchar(Str1, _, Rest),
    matchs(Rest, Str2, Size, Sub1).
```

Finally, this code reduces the source string by one character and calls itself recursively with the new string. This searching technique continues until a match is found or the end of the source string is encountered.

The previous two tools provide all of the capabilities needed for searching through strings; however, if you want to perform other string functions such as removing or inserting characters in strings, you need to develop other tools. Here is a tool which can be used for removing characters from a string:

```
/* The Strrightx Tool */

predicates
    strrightx(string, string, integer)      /* Extract right most chars */
    setparamr(integer, integer, integer)    /* Local Predicate    */

clauses
    strrightx(Srcstr, Trgstr, N_pos):-

        str_len(Srcstr, Size),              /* Get string length */
        setparamr(N_pos, Size, C_pos),      /* Determine char position */
        frontstr(C_pos, Srcstr,_, Trgstr) . /* Get right characters    */


    /* setparam tests for the error conditions and adjusts the
       character position to extract the right most characters from
       the source string.
    */

    setparamr(N_pos, Size, C_pos):-
        N_pos <= Size, N_pos >= 1,          /* character count okay */
        C_pos = N_pos - 1, ! .

    setparamr(N_pos, Size, C_pos):-
        N_pos > Size,                       /* position > size    */
        C_pos = Size - 1, ! .               /* return size        */

    setparamr(N_pos, _, C_pos):-
        N_pos < 1,                          /* position < 1       */
        C_pos = 0.                          /* return 0           */
```

This tool, strrightx, extracts the rightmost characters from a specified string starting at a specified location. If you specify such a goal:

```
strrightx("I wonder if the moon is round", Trg, 10).
```

the predicate returns with:

```
    Trg = "if the moon is round"
```

Strrightx is an extension of the built-in predicate, frontstr. The important addition is the error checking that this tool provides. The error checking is performed by the setparamr predicate. If you specify a number that is greater than or less than the string size, this predicate guarantees that a solution can be found. The error checking feature is important because it guarantees that this predicate will return a valid response back to the calling program.

The counterpart to this tool is strleftx which extracts the leftmost characters from a string:

```
/* The Strleftx Tool */

predicates

    strleftx(string, string, integer)       /* Extract left most chars */
    setparam(integer, integer, integer)     /* Local Predicate   */

clauses

    strleftx(Srcstr, Trgstr, N_char):-
        str_len(Srcstr, Size),                  /* Get string length */
        setparam(N_char, Size, C_count),        /* Determine count */
        frontstr(C_count, Srcstr, Trgstr,_).    /* Get left characters */

  /* setparam tests for the error conditions and adjusts the number of
     characters to extract from the source string.
  */

    setparam(N_char, Size, C_count):-
        N_char <= Size, N_char >= 1,            /* character count okay */
        C_count = N_char, ! .

    setparam(N_char, Size, C_count):-
        N_char > Size,                          /* count > size    */
        C_count = Size, ! .                     /* return size     */

    setparam(N_char, _, C_count):-
        N_char < 1,                             /* count < 1       */
        C_count = 0.                            /* return 0        */
```

Again, this tool performs the necessary error checking by using an internal predicate. Strleftx is useful for performing tasks such as removing the trailing blanks from a string. For example, the goal:

```
strleftx("Hello  ", 5, X).
```

produces the new string:

```
X = "Hello"
```

The two previous tools can be combined to create a string tool for extracting a group of characters from the middle of a string. This new tool is written as:

```
/* The Strmidx Tool */

include "strleftx.pro"
include "strrightx.pro"


predicates

    strmidx(string, string, integer, integer)   /* Extract mid characters */

clauses

    strmidx(Srcstr, Trgstr, C_pos, N_char):-

        strrightx(Srcstr, Tmpstr, C_pos),
        strleftx(Tmpstr, Trgstr, N_char).
```

Note that the two tools are included with Turbo Prolog's "include" statement. Of course, these tools could also be placed in one file and thus could be included as one unit. Strmidx contains four parameters. The first two parameters contain the source and target strings respectively and the third and fourth parameters contain the following values:

```
C_pos  - The starting position in the source string
           for character extraction.
N_char - The number of characters to extract from the
           source string.
```

To use the tool, you can specify a goal such as:

```
strmidx("All Prolog programs are easy to read",
Trg, 5, 6).
```

and strmidx first will call strrightx with the following:

```
strrightx("All Prolog programs are easy to read",
Tmpstr, 5)
```

which produces the binding:

```
Tmpstr = "Prolog programs are easy to read"
```

thus, the call to strleftx consists of:

```
strleftx("Prolog  programs  are  easy  to  read",
Trgstr, 6)
```

which in turn produces the result:

```
Trg = Prolog
```

The three string extraction tools developed here are useful for many applications involving string processing such as pattern matching, expression parsing, or language processing. These tools can be used to perform tasks such as removing punctuation marks from sentences or deleting leading or trailing blanks from expressions. In the chapter on natural language processing, both the strrightx and the strleftx tools are used to help parse English sentences.

String Insertion

Another useful tool to have in your string handling library is one for string insertion. Here is a tool for inserting a substring in another string at a specified location:

```
/* The Strsi Tool */

predicates

    strsi(string, string, integer, string)   /* Insert substring at index */
    setparami(integer, integer, integer)

clauses

    strsi(Srcstr, Substr, Index, Trgstr):-
        str_len(Srcstr, Size),
        setparami(Index, Size, Pos), !,           /* set insert position */
        frontstr(Pos, Srcstr, S1, S2),
        concat(S1, Substr, Temp),
        concat(Temp, S2, Trgstr).
```

(continued)

```
/* Test for error conditions    */

setparami(Index, Size, Pos):-
      Index > 0, Index <= Size + 1,
      Pos = Index - 1.

setparami(Index, Size, Pos):-
      Index > Size + 1,
      Pos = Size + 1.

setparami(Index, _, Pos):-
      Index <= 0,
      Pos = 0.
```

In this tool, strsi, the four arguments are the source string, the sub-string to insert in the source string, the location where the sub-string is inserted, and the string to contain the result of the new string. Strsi consists of two parts: an error checking predicate, setparmi, and the body of strsi itself which uses two built-in predicates, frontstr and concat, to perform the string insertion.

The procedure used by strsi consists of determining the length of the source string, calculating the actual location for inserting the sub-string, dividing the source string into two separate strings, and building the resulting string by using the concat operator. As an example, if you specify the goal:

```
strsi("one three", "two ", 5, X).
```

the first step performed would be to calculate the length of "one three". Once this length is determined, the predicate setparmi is called which adjusts the insertion position. In this case, the version of setparmi used is:

```
setparami(Index, Size, Pos):-
    Index > 0, Index <= Size + 1,
    Pos = Index - 1.
```

Note that the position is one location less than the specified insertion index. This value is used by the next predicate, frontstr, to divide the source string into two new strings. In this example the call looks like:

```
frontstr(4, "one three", S1, S2)
```

thus, the result is:

S1 = "one "   and   S2 = "three"

Finally, the two concat predicates put the strings:

"one" "two" "three"

together to form the resulting string "one two three."

A variation of this tool is a predicate which performs the operation of inserting a specified number of characters in a string. This tool uses the previous predicate, strsi, to perform this function:

```
/* The Strci Tool */

include "strsi.pro"

predicates

    strci(string, char, integer, integer, string)     /* Insert character(s)
                                                           at index */
clauses
    strci(S3, _, _, 0, Trgstr):- Trgstr = S3, !.

    strci(Srcstr, Ch, Index, No, Trgstr):-

            N = No - 1,
            str_char(S1, Ch),
            strsi(Srcstr, S1, Index, S3),
            strci(S3, Ch, Index, N, Trgstr), !.
```

If you specify a goal, such as:

strci("Help Me", ' ', 5, 4, X).

the result would be:

X = "Help   Me"

In this tool, the first argument is the source string and the second argument is the character to be inserted in the source string. The third and fourth arguments are the insertion index and the number of characters to insert. Finally, the last argument contains the resulting string.

Once again, recursion is used in this string tool. Strci consists of two predicates. The first checks for the condition where the number of characters to insert in the string is zero. The second predicate inserts one character at a time and reduces the character count by one. In this respect, strci uses a controlled loop of the form:

```
While character_count <> 0 DO
   Insert character
   character_count = character_count - 1
```

Strci is a powerful tool that can be used as the foundation of another tool for justifying strings. This next tool, strpad, performs the functions of padding a string with a given character and justifying the string according to one of three specifications:

```
l = left justify
r = right justify
c = center string in field
```

The tool is included here:

```
/* The Strpad Tool */

include "strci.pro"

predicates

    strpad(string, integer, symbol, char, string)    /* pad string */

clauses

    strpad(Srcstr, Width, l, Ch, Trgstr):-           /* pad left */

        str_len(Srcstr, Size),
        Width > Size,
        Chno = Width - Size,
        Ipos = Size + 1,
        strci(Srcstr, Ch, Ipos, Chno, Trgstr), !.

    strpad(Srcstr, Width, r, Ch, Trgstr):-           /* pad right */

        str_len(Srcstr, Size),
        Width > Size,
        Chno = Width - Size,
        strci(Srcstr, Ch, 0, Chno, Trgstr), !.

    strpad(Srcstr, Width, c, Ch, Trgstr):-           /* pad center */

        str_len(Srcstr, Size),
        Width > Size,
        Chno = Width - Size,
        Lno = Chno div 2,
        Rno = Chno - Lno,
        Ipos = Size + 1,
        strci(Srcstr, Ch, Ipos, Rno, S1),
        strci(S1, Ch, 0, Lno, Trgstr), !.
```

This tool contains five parameters, which are:

```
Srcstr - The source string
Width  - Length of justified string
Option - The justification option
Ch     - The pad character
Trgstr - The target string
```

The "Option" parameter allows you to specify one of three types of string justifications. The options are "l" for left justification, "r" for right justification, and "c" for center justification. An example of each operation is shown here.

Left Justification:

```
strpad("String", 12, l, "x", S).
```

which produces:

```
S = Stringxxxxxx
```

Right Justification:

```
strpad("String", 12, r, "x", S).
```

which produces:

```
S = xxxxxxString
```

Center Justification:

```
strpad("String", 12, c, "x", S).
```

which produces:

```
S = xxxStringxxx
```

Strpad is composed of three clauses. The first clause tests for the left justification option, the second clause tests for the right justification option, and the third clause tests for the center justification option. Tools created in this modular fashion have two advantages. First, you can easily test out each section while the tool is under development. Secondly, you can easily add other options to the tool to increase its performance.

Deleting Strings

The next string tools presented in this section are used for deleting characters and sub-strings from strings. The first tool, strcd, deletes n characters from a string starting at a specified location:

```
/* The Strcd Tool */

predicates

    strcd(string, integer, integer, string)     /* delete chars at index */
    setparamd(integer, integer, integer)

clauses

    strcd(Srcstr, Index, No, Trgstr):-

        str_len(Srcstr, Size),
        setparamd(Index, Size, Pos), !,          /* set insert position */
        frontstr(Pos, Srcstr, First, Rest),
        frontstr(No, Rest, _, S2),
        concat(First, S2, Trgstr).

    /* Test for error conditions   */

    setparamd(Index, Size, Pos):-

        Index > 0, Index <= Size + 1,
        Pos = Index - 1.

    setparamd(Index, Size, Pos):-

        Index > Size ,
        Pos = Size .

    setparamd(Index, _, Pos):-

        Index <= 0,
        Pos = 0.
```

As you can see, strcd is constructed like the tool strsi. It determines the length of the source string, checks for error conditions, divides the source string into two new strings, removes the characters from one of the new strings, and then
puts the two strings back together to form the resulting
string. If you specify the goal:

```
    strcd("Stringggggg", 7, 5, X).
```

where the arguments represent, in order, the source string,
the index, the number of characters to delete, and the resulting string, strcd produces:

```
    X = "String"
```

Strcd can now be used as the foundation of a tool for deleting a sub-string from a string.

Here is the new tool:

```
/* The Strsd Tool */

include "strsfind.pro"
include "strcd.pro"

predicates

    strsd(string, string, string)           /* delete substring */

clauses

    strsd(Srcstr, Substr, Trgstr):-

            strsfind(Srcstr, Substr, Pos),     /* get position */
            str_len(Substr, Size),
            strcd(Srcstr, Pos, Size, Trgstr).
```

This predicate, strsd, actually uses two tools developed in this section, strsfind and strcd. When you specify a goal, such as:

```
strsd("baseball", "base", X).
```

strsd first calls strsfind to find the location of the sub-string "base" in the source string "baseball." Once this position is determined, the length of the sub-string is calculated and strcd is called to perform the operation of deleting the sub-string. The result of this operation is:

```
X = "ball"
```

Tools such as strcd are powerful and easy to develop because they can be constructed from other tools. In fact, you could easily add more useful tools to the ones built in this section. For example, you might want to create a predicate for replacing characters or sub-strings in a string. In the next section, a few tools for replacing characters and sub-strings in strings are developed using insert, delete, and find tools developed in earlier sections.

Replacing Characters and Strings

The first tool that can be created with some of the previous tools is strcr. This string tool replaces a character in a given string with a specified number of characters. Here is the tool:

```
/* The Strcr Tool  */

include "strcd.pro"

include "strci.pro"

predicates

    strcr(string, char, integer, integer, string)   /* replace characters */

clauses

    strcr(Srcstr, Ch, Pos, Num, Trgstr):-

            strcd(Srcstr, Pos, 1, Tmpstr),
            strci(Tmpstr, Ch, Pos, Num, Trgstr).
```

Note that strcr performs the character replacement with calls
to strcd and strci. If you specify a goal such as:

```
    strcr("Hello World", 'X', 6, 5, Trg).
```

the tool performs the character replacement by calling strcd
with:

```
    strcd("Hello World", 6, 1, Tmpstr)
```

which produces:

```
    Tmpstr = HelloWorld
```

Thus the final call is:

```
    strci("HelloWorld", 'X', 6, 5, Trgstr)
```

and the final result is:

```
    Trgstr = HelloXXXXXWorld
```

The counterpart for strcr is a tool for replacing sub-strings
in a string. This tool, called strcr, is shown next:

```
/* The Strsr Tool */

include "strsfind.pro"
include "strcd.pro"
include "strsi.pro"

predicates

    strsr(string, string, string, string)     /* replace substring */
```

```
clauses

    strsr(Srcstr, Substr, Newstr, Trgstr):-

        strsfind(Srcstr, Substr, Pos),        /* get position */
        str_len(Substr, Size),
        strcd(Srcstr, Pos, Size, Tmpstr),
        strsi(Tmpstr, Newstr, Pos, Trgstr).
```

The parameters used in strsr are:

```
Srcstr — The source string
Substr — The sub-string to be replaced
Newstr — The new string to replace the sub-string with
Trgstr — The target string
```

In addition to using an insert and delete tool, strsr uses strsfind to locate the position of the sub-string specified for replacement. For example, if you specify the goal:

```
strsr("The man is programming", "man", "lady", Trg).
```

strsfind first attempts to locate the position of the sub-string "man." Of course, if this sub-string is not found, the goal fails. In our example, however, the sub-string is located and the final result is:

```
Trgstr = The lady is programming
```

Additional String Tools

The final tools created in this section are used to compare strings. Although Turbo Prolog allows you to compare strings with the operators "=," "<," and ">," it is worthwhile to build a tool that combines all of these operations. Strcmp tests two strings and returns a code to reflect the results of the comparison. For each comparison, one of the following codes are returned:

```
R_code = 0   strings are equal
R_code = 1   string 1 > string 2
R_code = -1  string 1 < string 2
```

The tool itself contains three clauses for testing the two strings:

```
/* The Strcmp Tool */

predicates
  strcmp(string, string, integer)
  strchk(string, string, integer)

clauses
    strcmp(Str1, Str2, R_code):-
        strchk(Str1, Str2, R_code).

    strchk(Str1,Str1, R):-
        R = 0, ! .

    strchk(Str1,Str2, R):-
        Str1 > Str2, R = 1, !.

    strchk(Str1,Str2, R):-
        Str1 < Str2, R = -1.
```

As shown, the string comparison is performed by strchk. Because this tool handles all possible cases, it can be used to sort strings in alphabetical order. For example, if you call strcmp with the following:

```
strcmp("Alpha", "Beta", R)
```

the return code "R" is assigned a value of –1 indicating that the first string should precede the second string.

A variation of strcmp is created by using a tool which compares the first n characters of two strings. This tool also uses the same return codes as strcmp:

```
/* The Strncmp Tool */

include "strleftx.pro"

predicates

  strncmp(string, string, integer, integer)
  strchk(string, string, integer)

clauses

    strncmp(Str1, Str2, Nchar, R_code):-

        strleftx(Str1, S1, Nchar),
        strleftx(Str2, S2, Nchar),
        strchk(S1, S2, R_code).
```

```
strchk(Str1,Str1, R):-
    R = 0, ! .

strchk(Str1,Str2, R):-
    Str1 > Str2, R = 1, !.

strchk(Str1,Str2, R):-
    Str1 < Str2, R = -1.
```

Note that this tool uses strleftx to extract the specified number of characters from both strings for the comparison. Once this operation is performed, strncmp makes a call to strchk to compare the sub-strings. A goal such as:

```
strncmp("grandstand", "grandparent", 5, R)
```

produces the result:

```
R = 0
```

because the first five characters of each string are equivalent.

If you wanted to extend the capabilities of this tool, you could write a clause to compare the last n characters of two strings. To perform this task, the tool strrightx should be used in place of strleftx.

Lists with Turbo Prolog

Lists are an important data type in Turbo Prolog. Many useful tools can be created to perform operations on lists such as searching for elements in a list, appending two lists, deleting elements from a list, and inserting elements in a list. Lists are traditionally used in AI programs as a form of knowledge representation. In this section, you will learn how to write some general purpose list tools with Turbo Prolog.

Lists can be represented with any of the five basic data types:

```
character
integer
real
string
symbol
```

In one respect, you can consider the string type in Turbo Prolog to be a form of a list of characters. Thus, all of the string handling tools developed in the previous section can be easily represented as list tools. Of course the advantage of the list representation is that it provides you with a more general data structure.

The first tool developed here is used to search for an element in a list. This predicate, called member, is shown here:

```
/* The Simple Member Tool */

domains

    sylist = symbol*

predicates

    member( symbol,  sylist, integer )

clauses

    member( Token, [ Token | _ ], 1 ).

    member( Token, [ _ | Rest ], Position ) :-
        !, member( Token, Rest,      Cur_position ),
        Position = Cur_position + 1.
```

This tool searches a list for an element and returns the position of the element in the list, if found. For example, if you specify the goal:

```
member(saul, [john, tom, saul, eric], Pos).
```

the member predicate returns:

```
Pos = 3
```

In member, the first predicate tests to see if the element you are searching for is the first element of the list. If this is not the case, the second predicate is called. This predicate steps through the list using recursion. Each member of the list is compared to the element you are searching for until the element is found or the end of the list is encountered.

The problem with the member predicate is that it only accepts lists of the symbol's data type. If you attempted to search a list of strings or integers, the tool would fail because of a type mismatch. To improve the tool, you can add more domains. Here is the new version of member:

```
/* A General Purpose Member */

domains

    clist = char*
    ilist = integer*
    rlist = real*
    slist = string*
    sylist = symbol*

predicates

    member( char,    clist, integer )      /* Member of character list.    */
    member( integer, ilist, integer )      /* Member of integer list.      */
    member( real,    rlist, integer )      /* Member of real list.         */
    member( string,  slist, integer )      /* Member of string list.       */
    member( symbol,  sylist, integer )     /* Member of symbol list.       */

clauses

    member( Token, [ Token | _ ], 1 ).

    member( Token, [ _ | Rest ], Position ) :-
        !, member( Token, Rest, Cur_position ),
        Position = Cur_position + 1.
```

Note the addition of the definitions for the member predicate. This tool now supports all five of the standard Turbo Prolog data types. You can now use a list of any one of these data types with this tool. Even though Turbo Prolog is a typed language, you can still construct general tools which will work with different data types. The only constraint is that all of the elements of a given list must be of the same type.

Joining Lists

The second list tool that you should add to your toolbox is append. This tool joins two lists together and creates a new list. Here is the code:

```
/* The Append Tool */

domains

    clist = char*
    ilist = integer*
    rlist = real*
    slist = string*
    sylist = symbol*
```

(continued)

```
predicates
    append( clist, clist, clist )      /* Append 2 charater lists.   */
    append( ilist, ilist, ilist )      /* Append 2 integer lists.    */
    append( rlist, rlist, rlist )      /* Append 2 real lists.       */
    append( slist, slist, slist )      /* Append 2 string lists.     */
    append( sylist, sylist, sylist )   /* Append 2 symbol lists.     */

clauses

    append([ ], List, List ).

    append([ Head | List1 ], List2, [ Head | Rest ] ) :-
        append( List1, List2, Rest ), !.
```

Append uses three arguments. The first two arguments store the two lists that are appended and the third argument contains the result of this operation. For example, the goal:

```
append([a,b], [c,d], X).
```

produces:

```
X = [a,b,c,d].
```

As an added bonus, this tool can be used in other ways. Here are some examples:

```
1. append([a,b], X, [a,b,c,d])      X = [c,d]

2. append(X, [c,d], [a,b,c,d])      X = [a,b]

3. append([a,b], [c,d], [a,b,c,d])  True
```

The first example shows that the append predicate can find a list to join at the end of another list (the first list) to create the final list. The second example is similar to the first except that here the append finds the first list. Finally, the last example illustrates that the append predicate can be used to verify that two lists, when appended, create the specified resulting list.

If you look at the code closely, you will notice that this predicate also uses recursion. In fact, all of the list tools presented in this section use recursion to manipulate lists. Append contains two parts. The first append predicate looks for the case where the first list is empty. The other predicate contains the recursion as shown:

```
append([ Head | List1 ], List2, [ Head | Rest ] ):-
    append( List1, List2, Rest ), !.
```

Here the first element or head of the first list is placed at the beginning of the third list. The append predicate then calls itself with the three arguments: List1, List2, and Rest. List1 contains the original first list except the first element. List2 does not change; it always contains the original second list. Finally, Rest stores the new list to be constructed. To further understand how the recursion is used in this predicate, you should study the following example. Assume you want to append the two lists:

```
[1,2] and [3,4]
```
Therefore, your goal is:

```
append([1,2], [3,4], X).
```
The first predicate, append([], List, List), will fail because the first list is not empty. When the second predicate is called, the results of this first call are:

```
Call 1:
        Head  = [1]
        List1 = [2]
        List2 = [3,4]
```
Now the body of the predicate is executed resulting in:

```
append([2], [3,4], Rest)
```
The recursion begins here and the next call to append results in:

```
Call 2:
        Head  = [2]
        List1 = []
        List2 = [3,4]
```
This time, the new call is:

```
append([], [3,4], Rest)
```
Note here that the first list is now empty. This condition causes the first append clause to be matched. Therefore, the outcome of this operation is:

```
Rest = [3,4]
```
Because the append predicate has now succeeded, backtracking will occur. The first step is a return to call 2 where Head is joined with Rest to form the new result:

```
Rest = [2,3,4]
```

Finally, the return to call 1 produces:

```
Rest = [1,2,3,4]
```

Building Additional List Tools

The two tools presented in the previous sections, member and append, serve as the two fundamental list handling tools used in most applications which use lists. In this section additional list tools are created for performing tasks such as deleting members from a list, determining the length of a list, and reversing the elements of a list.

Here is a predicate for deleting a member from a list:

```
/* The Delete Tool */


domains

    clist = char*
    ilist = integer*
    rlist = real*
    slist = string*
    sylist = symbol*

predicates

    delete( char,    clist, clist ) /* Delete character from list.      */
    delete( integer, ilist, ilist )         /* Delete integer from list.      */
    delete( real,    rlist, rlist )         /* Delete real from list.         */
    delete( string,  slist, slist )         /* Delete string from list.       */
    delete( symbol,  sylist, sylist )       /* Delete symbol from list.       */

clauses

    delete( _, [ ], [ ] ).

    delete( Head, [ Head | Tail ], Tail ) :- !.

    delete( Token, [ Head | Tail ], [ Head | Result ] ) :- !,
        delete( Token, Tail, Result ).
```

Delete removes only the first occurrence of a specified element from a list. For example, the goal:

```
delete(b, [a,b,b,c,d], X).
```

would produce the new list:

```
X = [a,b,c,d].
```

This predicate contains three arguments: the element to be deleted, the list to perform the operation on, and the resulting list. Delete can also be called with different bindings for the three arguments to produce results such as:

```
delete( b, X, [ a, c ] )              X = [ b, a, c]
delete( X, [ a, b, c ], [ a, c ] )   X = b
delete( b, [ a, b, c ], [ a, c ] )   True
```

One variation of the delete predicate is a tool for deleting all occurrences of an element from a list. Here is the code:

```
/* The Delete_all Tool */


clauses

    delete_all( _, [ ], [ ] ).

    delete_all( Head, [ Head | Tail ], Result ) :- !,
        delete_all( Head, Tail,     Result ).

    delete_all( Token, [ Head | Tail ], [ Head | Result ] ) :- !,
        delete_all( Token, Tail, Result ).
```

Note that the domain and predicate declarations have been omitted this time. In order to make this a complete predicate, you should add the definitions from the previous delete predicate. With this tool, if you specify a goal such as:

```
delete_all(a, [a,c,b,a,d,a], X).
```

the new list would be:

```
X = [c,b,d]
```

Another tool worth having in your toolbox of basic list handling predicates is list_length. As its name implies, this predicate determines the length of a list:

```
/* The List_length Tool */

predicates

    list_length( clist, integer )    /* Length of character list.  */
    list_length( ilist, integer )    /* Length of integer list.    */
    list_length( rlist, integer )    /* Length of real list.       */
```

(continued)

```
      list_length( slist, integer )      /* Length of string list.      */
      list_length( sylist, integer )     /* Length of symbol list.      */

clauses

   list_length( [ ], 0 ).

   list_length( [ _ | Tail ], Size ) :- !,
      list_length( Tail, Old_Size ),
      Size = Old_Size + 1.
```

Note again that the domains section has been omitted. You can add the domain definition from the previously constructed list tools to complete this predicate. List_length consists of two parts: a predicate which looks for the case of the empty list and a predicate which uses recursion to step through the list. The recursive predicate calls itself until the first predicate succeeds (the end of the list is encountered) and then when the recursive calls unwind, the list counter argument, Size, is updated to reflect the length of the list.

The next list tool developed uses the append predicate. This tool reverses the elements of a list. For example, if you specify the goal:

```
   reverse([a,b,c,d,e], X).
```

this tool will create the new list:

```
   X = [e,d,c,b,a]
```

Here is the code for reverse:

```
/* The Reverse Tool */

include "append.pro"

predicates

      reverse( clist, clist )     /* Reverse the character list.   */
      reverse( ilist, ilist )     /* Reverse the integer list.     */
      reverse( rlist, rlist )     /* Reverse the real list.        */
      reverse( slist, slist )     /* Reverse the string list.      */
      reverse( ylist, ylist )     /* Reverse the symbol list.      */

clauses

      reverse( [ ], [ ] ).
```

```
reverse( [ Head | Tail ], Result ) :- !,
    reverse( Tail, Temp ),
    append( Temp, [ Head ], Result ).
```

As shown, reverse calls itself, removing one element at a time from the source list. When the list is empty, the first reverse predicate succeeds:

```
reverse( [ ], [ ] ).
```

and the append operator takes over as the recursion unwinds.

The last tool developed is called unique. Unique removes the duplicate elements from a list. For example, the list:

```
[1,2,3,4,5,1,2,4,6,10]
```

would result in the new list:

```
[1,2,3,4,5,6,10]
```

where the duplicate elements have been removed. The code for unique is:

```
/* The Unique Tool */

include "member.pro"                    /* Include the member predicate */

predicates

    unique( clist, clist )      /* Strip the character list.    */
    unique( ilist, ilist )      /* Strip the integer list.      */
    unique( rlist, rlist )      /* Strip the real list.         */
    unique( slist, slist )      /* Strip the string list.       */
    unique( sylist, sylist )    /* Strip the symbol list.       */

clauses

    unique( [ ], [ ] ).

    unique( [ Head | Tail ], Result ) :-
        member( Head, Tail, _ ), !,
        unique( Tail, Result ).

    unique( [ Head | Tail ], [ Head | Result ] ) :-
        unique( Tail, Result ).
```

This tool contains three predicates. The first one again looks for the case where both lists are empty. The second unique predicate uses the member predicate to check for duplicate elements in the list. Finally, the last predicate recursively calls itself and moves the first element of the source list to the first element of the target list. Unique uses essentially the same technique found in the other list tools which consists of reducing a list by one member at a time until the end of the list is reached.

Working with Strings and Lists

In some cases, it is useful to combine both string and list operations. For example, if you wanted to build a tool for reversing the characters in a string, one approach would be to convert the string into a list of characters, reverse the list and then convert the list back into a string. The following tool performs this operation:

```
/* The Strrev Tool */

domains
  symlist = symbol*

predicates
  strrev(string, string)
  buildlist(string, symlist)
  reverse(symlist, symlist)
  append(symlist, symlist, symlist)

clauses
  strrev(Srcstr, Trgstr):-

      buildlist(Srcstr, List1),
      reverse(List1, List2),
      buildlist(Trgstr, List2).

  buildlist("", []):- ! .

  buildlist(Str, [First | Tail]):-
      bound(Str),
      frontstr(1, Str, First, Rest),
      buildlist(Rest, Tail).

  buildlist(Str, [First | Tail]):-
      free(Str),
      bound(First),
      buildlist(Rest, Tail),
      concat(First, Rest, Str).

      reverse([], []).
      reverse([A|B], C):-
        reverse(B, D), append(D, [A], C).
```

```
append([A|B], C, [A|D]):- append(B, C, D).
append([], X, X).
```

The clause, buildlist, is responsible for converting a string into a list and converting a list into a string. For example, if the clause contains the arguments:

```
buildlist("John", L)
```

the result is:

```
L = [J,o,h,n]
```

On the other hand, if the following arguments are provided:

```
buildlist(S, [J,o,h,n])
```

the clause returns:

```
S = John
```

Buildlist is a recursive clause consisting of three parts. The first:

```
buildlist("", []):- ! .
```

tests the arguments for the terminating condition where the first argument is the empty string and the second argument is the empty list. This condition forces the recursion to terminate. The second part of buildlist, coded as:

```
buildlist(Str, [First | Tail]):-
    bound(Str),
    frontstr(1, Str, First, Rest),
    buildlist(Rest, Tail).
```

performs the conversion of a string into a list. Note that the built-in predicate, bound, is used to determine if the argument "Str" is assigned a value. If this condition is true, buildlist continues to convert the string into a list by using recursive calls.

The final part of buildlist converts a list into a string:

```
buildlist(Str, [First | Tail]):-
        free(Str),
        bound(First),
        buildlist(Rest, Tail),
        concat(First, Rest, Str).
```

Note that, in this case, the free predicate is used to determine if the conversion is from a list to a string. The recursion continues until the end of the list is encountered and then the built-in concat predicate constructs the new string.

The reverse tool is called with two arguments: the first argument contains the source string and the second argument stores the result. For example, the goal:

```
reverse("one two three", Trg)
```

produces:

```
Trg = eerht owt eno
```

To see how the reverse predicate can be applied to a useful application, take a look at the following tool:

```
/* The Strslfind Tool */

include "strrev.pro"
include "strsfind.pro"

predicates

    strslfind(string, string, integer)    /* Search for last substring
                                              in string */

clauses

    strslfind(Srcstr, Substr, Pos):-

        strrev(Srcstr, Trgstr),            /* reverse string    */
        str_len(Srcstr, Size),             /* get length of string   */
        str_len(Substr, Ssize),            /* get length of substring */
        strrev(Substr, S1),
        strsfind(Trgstr, S1, I),           /* check for string match */
        Pos = Size - (Ssize + I) + 2.      /* update position   */
```

This tool, strslfind, looks for the last occurrence of sub-string in a string. To perform this operation, the tool first reverses the source string and then uses the tool strsfind to find the first occurrence of the sub-string. The index position of the sub-string is adjusted to represent the position of the last occurrence of the sub-string.

Another useful tool that works with both lists and strings is strslist. This tool looks for a match between a list of substrings and a string. For example, you can provide the tool with a list such as:

```
["fun", "run", "walk"]
```

and a string such as:

"The man is running on the beach"

and the tool finds a match with the sub-string "run" and the word "running."

The code for this tool is shown here:

```
/* The Strslist Tool */

include "strsfind.pro"

domains

    slist = string*

predicates

    strslist(string, slist, integer, string)
    getsmem(slist, string)
    remvmem(slist, slist)


clauses

    strslist(_, [], _, _):-
        fail, !.

    strslist(Srcstr, List, Pos, Matchstr):-

        getsmem(List, S1),
        strsfind(Srcstr, S1, Pos),
        Matchstr = S1, !.

    strslist(Srcstr, List, Pos, Matchstr):-

        remvmem(List, L1),
        strslist(Srcstr, L1, Pos, Matchstr), !.

    getsmem([H|_], H).

    remvmem([_|T], T).
```

Strslist takes four arguments which are in order:

```
Srcstr   — The source string
List     — The list of sub-strings to match with
           the source string
Pos      — The position of the match between a sub-
           string from the list and the source
           string
Matchstr — The matching sub-string
```

The last tool built in this chapter is similar to strslist. This tool, strclist, looks for a match between a list of characters and a string. The tool is written as:

```
/* The Strclist Tool */

include "strcfind.pro"

domains

    clist = char*

predicates

    strclist(string, clist, integer, char)
    getcmem(clist, char)
    remvmem(clist, clist)


clauses

    strclist(_, [], _, _):-
        fail, !.

    strclist(Srcstr, List, Pos, Matchchar):-

        getcmem(List, Ch),
        strcfind(Srcstr, Ch, Pos),
        Matchchar = Ch, !.

    strclist(Srcstr, List, Pos, Matchchar):-

    remvmem(List, L1),
    strclist(Srcstr, L1, Pos, Matchchar), !.

getcmem([H|_], H).

remvmem([_|T], T).
```

In strclist, all of the arguments are similar to the arguments in strslist; however, the second argument must be represented as a character list. Thus an example calling sequence for this tool would be:

```
strclist("Tom", ['a', 'e', 'i', 'o', 'u'], P, M).
```

which produces the results:

```
P = 2
M = o
```

Using the Tools

Many of the tools developed in this chapter can be combined so that you can create useful libraries. For example, you could put all of the string processing tools in one file and include this file in other programs. Since some tools use other tools, this would eliminate the problem of leaving out a tool or including the wrong one. All of the tools presented in this chapter can be extended and used as the foundation for other more complex tools. You might find it helpful to work with these tools in their present form and add to them to create a powerful library of tools to support your own programming needs.

CHAPTER 4

Reasoning with Machines—The Inference Engine

Any brain, machine or other thing that has a mind must be composed of smaller things that cannot think at all.
—**Marvin Minsky**

The real challenge for an AI programmer is to develop programs that can "think" or reason with the complexity of human reasoning. For one thing, the amount of information that must be put into the computer is enormous. Think about the vast amounts of knowledge you acquired during childhood, at school, and through other life experiences. It would probably take longer to put all this information into the computer than it took to acquire it. Programming the computer to reason is complicated further because the human reasoning process is not well understood. After all, no two people reason about a situation or experience in exactly the same way.

Over the centuries, mathematicians and philosophers have been developing systems of logic and other models to represent the reasoning process. Some of these systems now serve as the foundation for developing programs that simulate human reasoning. In this chapter, some of these important systems and concepts are introduced and in the final section you will use these concepts to develop a useful inference engine.

What Is Reasoning?

Some mathematicians and philosophers have defined reasoning as a process of categorizing information in the form of known facts, rules, and partial knowledge, and creating new facts and rules. An example of this reasoning process is shown in Figure 4.1.

Assume you are given the two facts shown in Box A. Using a simple reasoning process, you could conclude the new fact in Box C. This reasoning process could consist of applying the following rule: "If X is a computer and all computers have memory, then X has memory." Thus, you are starting with two known facts and inferring a new fact by applying a simple rule. This process is easy to understand. Unfortunately, not all reasoning processes are this simple. The reasoning process that you might follow to solve most problems usually depends on a number of things. First, the problem type and complexity must be considered. Sometimes an estimate, based on experience, or a "quick guess," will solve a simple problem. For example, deciding how much money to pay the babysitter is a good case of this simple reasoning process. Paying the IRS the correct amount at tax time, on the other hand, is not so simple because it requires reading, reviewing, and extensive analysis. Another thing affecting the reasoning process is the accuracy, depth, and nature of the knowledge required to solve a problem. The seasoned CPA can easily follow the IRS forms because of his or her experience—knowledge base. The reasoning process also may be affected by an emotional bias. In the tax example, the answers calculated by taxpayers may be biased by their feelings about paying large sums of money to the IRS.

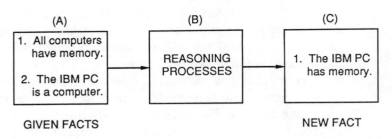

Figure 4.1   A Simple Reasoning Process

To help you understand some of the important reasoning processes that people use, a few techniques including reasoning by analogy, common sense reasoning, meta-level reasoning, and formal reasoning, are presented next.

Reasoning by Analogy

Knowledge accumulated from past experiences is often used in a comparative way to help you form new conclusions. For example, assume you are about to water-ski in a new lake and you are wondering if you should wear a wet suit. You reason that yesterday the water at another lake was very cold and you needed a wet suit. You know that both of these lakes are in the same region and the temperature hasn't changed. Therefore, you conclude that the new lake will also be cold and that you will need a wet suit. Without any hard facts, such as the temperature of the lake, you have reached a decision.

This next example of reasoning by analogy should be a familiar one; it is often used in intelligence tests. In Figure 4.2 you are given two geometric objects which are related by a simple relationship.

In diagram 1, a box is drawn around a small circle in the upper half of the diagram. The lower half of the diagram contains a smaller square. In diagram 2, the box is removed from the circle and is placed around the square. Now, given this relationship, see if you can determine which of the Figure 4.3 diagrams B through E are related to diagram A in the same way that diagram 2 is related to 1 in Figure 4.2.

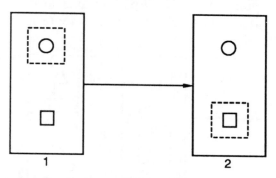

Figure 4.2   Relationship Between Geometric Objects

In Figure 4.3, instead of a box around the upper circle in diagram A, there is a triangle. The corresponding diagram is the one with the triangle placed around the lower square—diagram E. Therefore A and E in Figure 4.3 represent the same relationship as shown by 1 and 2 in Figure 4.2.

As you can imagine, there are a number of difficult hurdles to overcome if you attempt to write a program to solve such geometric reasoning problems. The first step is to determine a method for putting the information that describes the geometric figures into a representation that the computer could manipulate. Even if you use only primary shapes such as circles, squares, and triangles, this is still a difficult task. Next comes the definition of the possible transformations from the initial to final drawing. These include the shifting, rotating, expanding, contracting, and inverting of figures. Also, you must specify the relative positions as well as the concepts of inside, outside, and overlapping. Finally, you must develop the strategy that determines the relationship between the first two figures. Once the relationship is determined, it must then be tested on the second set of candidates. This type of reasoning is still very difficult for computers to do in general.

Common Sense Reasoning

This is probably the most natural process of reasoning for people and the most difficult process for computers. Teaching a computer common sense requires enormous amounts of knowledge. Your day to day experiences, over the course of your life, make up the basis for your common sense reasoning. Thus, if you wanted to program common sense into a

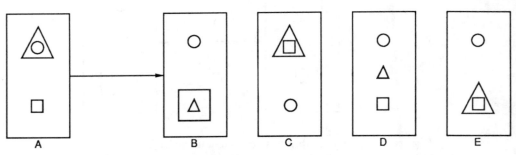

Figure 4.3   Can You Find the Correct Relationship?

computer, the underlying question is: how can you put that much information in a computer? Research continues on this interesting aspect of reasoning but tools or techniques to accomplish this are still not readily available for personal computers.

Perhaps this example will help you see some of the problems with teaching a computer common sense. Assume that you have taught a robot to ride a bicycle around the floor in a test laboratory. In learning to ride the bicycle, it has mastered the tasks of balancing, starting, stopping, and turning. It knows not to run into such obstacles as lab walls, tables, and chairs. The robot can also go from a specified starting location in the lab to a specific destination.

Now it is time for the robot to earn its keep, so you instruct it to deliver a package across town. After leaving the lab, it rides the bike down the stairs. After you carry it back to the laboratory for major repairs, the stairs are added to its obstacles list. The robot didn't have any stairs in the laboratory so it didn't know about them. On its second venture, it runs into a moving car—there were no moving objects, such as cars, in the lab. You now instruct it about the virtues of avoiding any objects, especially ones that are moving. On its third venture, it ends up in a ditch, trying to avoid a butterfly that had flown in its path. At this point, you are about ready to give up on the robot.

This example may sound silly to anyone with some level of common sense, but imagine a computer that has no way of learning unless you give it all of the information it needs to make intelligent decisions.

Meta-Level Reasoning

Meta-level reasoning is another process you use to make day-to-day decisions. This form of reasoning concerns your ability to relate to and understand experiences using the extent of your knowledge. An example should clarify how this process works.

After spending years working with the IBM PC, you might feel quite confident in your ability to answer most general questions about this personal computer. You become self-assured because you have a good understanding about the PC. In other words, you feel your knowledge about the PC is complete. Probably you are also aware of the areas where your knowledge is incomplete. If someone asks you a question about the Macintosh, which is outside your area of expertise, you realize your knowledge is not as complete and you will not be as confident. Here, you are analyzing your knowledge and experience level in terms of its depth, reliability, and so forth. You are thinking about your own thinking process. This meta-level is one step above the normal reasoning process. Although research is being done in this area, no real tools or techniques are available today with the power and flexibility of meta-level reasoning.

Formal Reasoning

Formal reasoning was first pursued by the ancient Greek philosophers in their quest to understand reasoning and knowledge. It evolved into the mathematical and philosophical study of logic. You were probably taught many of the principles of formal reasoning when you studied math or logic in school. The foundation of logic (formal reasoning) is based on the concept of truth. In formal logic, a statement is either true or false. This system of logic is related to the logic of computers, which is based on the binary system. Formal reasoning involves the use of pre-defined rules of logic that manipulate data to generate new rules and data. There are two primary examples of this type of formal reasoning: propositional calculus and predicate calculus. Both of these are presented in the next two sections. In case you are wondering, neither of these forms of logic deal with the calculus that is taught in mathematics.

Propositional Calculus

Propositional calculus or propositional logic, as it is more commonly called, is a system of formal logic based on a simple set of operators and statements. A proposition is a statement that can have either a true or false truth value. Such propositions can be used to represent real-world facts. Here are some propositions:

- Bill Cosby is a comedian
- PC AT's use the 286 processor
- Twelve plus seven equals nineteen

Partial statements such as "is a comedian" or "PC AT's use" are not propositions because they cannot be assigned a truth value. Propositional logic is useful for simulating reasoning because it is simple in structure and provides a flexible tool for handling decisions.

To combine propositions into more interesting and useful propositions, there are operations that you can use. In propositional logic, these operators are called conjunctive or combinational operators. They are shown in Table 4.1.

Table 4.1   Definition of the Conjunctive Operators

English Symbol	Logic Symbol	Meaning
And	&	A & B is true if A = true and B = true else A & B is false
Or	V	A V B is true if A = true or B = true else A V B is false
Implies	-->	A --> B is true if A is true or B is false If A is true then B must be true
Equivalent	==	A == B is true if both A and B are true or both A and B are false A== B is false if A and B have different values
Not	!	!A is true if A is false !A is false if A is true

The A and B symbols are propositional variables. They can be assigned the value of true or false. For example, a statement such as, "After you clean your room and do your chores, you can go to the ballgame" can be written:

```
A & B -> C
```

where A represents the phrase "clean your room," B represents "do your chores," and C represents "go to the ballgame." If this logic statement is constructed as:

```
A V B -> C
```

you might not do both chores because you are given a choice between doing your chores and cleaning your room.

The following truth table may help you remember the definitions of the operators.

Table 4.2   Truth Table Definition of the Conjunctive Operators

A	B	A & B	A V B	A —> B	A == B	!A
T	T	T	T	T	T	F
T	F	F	T	F	F	F
F	T	F	T	T	F	T
F	F	F	F	T	T	T

The truth table is useful for helping you to understand the possible results of a proposition. As an example, Table 4.2 provides all possible results of the conjunctive operators. The first two columns, from the left, show the states of the variables A and B. The combinations of propositions to be tested are shown at the top of the table and the actual truth values are inside the table. Note that the number of combinations for a single variable is two and the number for two variables is four. In case you haven't already guessed, the number of possible combinations goes up by the power of 2 to the nth power where n is the number of variables.

To better understand how the truth table is constructed, look at the case "A & B." In the first line, the leftmost column indicates that A is "T" and in the next column B is also "T." If you examine Table 4.1 you will notice that "T" and "T" is "T," thus a "T" is placed under the entry of "A & B"—sounds logical, right? This process continues until the entire table is filled out. Now, if you want to know the truth value of "True implies False," you can see in the table that it is false.

These propositions are combined to form expressions. And just as in algebra or geometry, there are statements that are always true. These identities are called *tautologies*. A commonly used tautology is:

```
(( A —> B ) & ( A —> C )) == ( A —> ( B & C ))
```

which states that the statement "A implies B and A implies C" is equivalent to the statement "A implies B and C." As an example, assume you have the following definitions:

```
A — RAINING B — CLOUDY C — GROUND IS WET
```

Therefore, the tautology becomes:

```
(( RAINING —> CLOUDY ) & ( RAINING —> GROUND IS WET ))
== ( RAINING —> ( CLOUDY & GROUND IS WET ))
```

Table 4.3   Truth Table Proof of the Propositional Tautology

			((A —> B) & (A —> C)) == (A —> (B & C))					
A	B	C	A—>B	A—>C	(4&5)	B&C	A—>(7)	(6)==(8)
(1)	(2)	(3)	(4)	(5)	(6)	(7)	(8)	9)
T	T	T	T	T	T	T	T	T
T	T	F	T	F	F	F	F	T
T	F	T	F	T	F	F	F	T
T	F	F	F	F	F	F	F	T
F	T	T	T	T	T	T	T	T
F	T	F	T	T	T	F	T	T
F	F	T	T	T	T	F	T	T
F	F	F	T	T	T	F	T	T

One way to prove a tautology is to use a truth table as shown in Table 4.3. Note that with three variables, there are eight cases. Also note the order of the cases in the first 3 columns on the left. The first half of the tautology is in columns 4, 5, and 6. The second half of the tautology is in columns 7 and 8. The results of the equivalence are in column 9. Since column 9 contains all true values, the statement is true and it is indeed a tautology.

Propositional calculus is important because it provides the foundation for rules of inference. As explained in Chapter 2, a rule of inference is a condition that is followed to transform a group of logical statements into a new group of statements. You can see that this new statement must be true if it is derived from statements that are true. The most popular inference rule is called *modus ponens*. Here is the general and formal definition:

```
Modus Ponens - General:      If A and A -> B are true
                             then you can infer B is
                             true.
             Formal:         ( A & ( A -> B )) -> B
```

And here is an example:

```
If you know the following two statements are true:
        1) When the car is running, the engine is hot.
        2) The car is running.
```

```
Then you know:
            The engine is hot.
```

This can be proven using the truth table approach explained above.

Often propositions can be transformed or reduced using tautologies or theorems. Translate, the following Turbo Prolog program, applies one level of translation to a given proposition. The output is a different, possibly reduced, proposition. This program has a simple but useful user interface, a parser, and an evaluator. The main clause is shown here:

```
translate :-
    makewindow(1,1,7,"Proposition",1,1,20,60),
    repeat,
    write("\n\nEnter Proposition or q to quit.\n: "),
    readln(Statement),
    parse(Statement, State_list),
    eval(State_list).
```

Translate is the clause that handles the user interface. It opens a window titled Proposition and then executes repeat. Repeat, is a tool described in Chapter 3. The readln statement asks you to enter either a preposition or "q" to terminate the program. Parse converts the string to a list of tokens or symbols and eval performs the conversion and prints the final answer.

The parse clause uses recursion to convert the entered string into individual tokens as shown:

```
parse("", []).
parse(Statement, [TokenList]) :-
        fronttoken(Statement,Token,Remainder),
        parse(Remainder,List).
```

First it checks for an empty string indicating that the parsing is completed. If the string is not empty, it uses the built-in Turbo Prolog predicate fronttoken to obtain the next leftmost token. A token is a string of one or more characters not containing any delimiters. The delimiters are space, the mathematical and inequality symbols, and the special characters such as carriage return and tab. Fronttoken returns the remainder of the string which is then used on the next recursive call to parse. The predicate fronttoken is not very useful for parsing propositional logic if symbols like "—>" or "==" are used. It treats each of the characters as separate tokens. Fronttoken can be replaced with the more flexible get_token, developed later in the book.

The eval clause is shown next:

```
eval(q).
eval(Statement) :-
    transform(State_list, Final_state, Reason),
    write("\nFinal Proposition = "),
    write_list(Final_state),
    write("\nReduced By - ", Reason),
    !, fail.
```

This clause first checks for a "q" indicating the program is over. Otherwise, it calls transform, which does the proposition conversion. If a translation is not needed, eval returns to the translate clause with a failure. If a translation is performed, then write_list is called to print the new proposition. Finally, a message which explains the translation process used is printed.

The heart of this program, the transform clause, is implemented as a look-up table:

```
transform(["not", "(", "not", "X", ")"],
          ["X"], "Reduce Double Negation") :- !.

transform(["X", "=", "Y"],
          ["not", "X", "v", "Y"],
          "Eliminate Implication") :- !.

transform(["not", "(", "X", "&", "Y", ")"],
          ["not", "X", "v", "not", "Y"],
          "De Morgan's Theorem for And") :- !.

transform(["not", "(", "X", "v", "Y", ")"],
          ["not", "X", "&", "not", "Y"],
          "De Morgan's Theorem for Or") :- !.

transform(["X", "&", "Y", "v", "Z"],
          [ "(", "X", "v", "Z", ")", "&",
          "(", "Y", "v", "Z", ")"],
          "Distribution") :-!.

transform(["X", "v", "Y", "&", "Z"],
          ["(", "X", "v", "Z", ")", "&",
          "(", "X", "v", "Z", ")"],
          "Distribution") :- !.
```

```
transform(_, [], "") :-
         write("\nInitial proposition was not
         transformed."), !, fail.
```

Turbo Prolog's unification mechanism is used to do the comparison between the proposition being checked and the ones in the table. If there is a match, the second argument is returned as the new proposition and the third argument contains the name of the theorem or the type of conversion used. On a match, the cut is used to eliminate further searches. If there are no matches, a message is sent indicating that no transformation was performed. Only a few of the propositional rules and theorems are included here to demonstrate the concept.

The final clause in this program is write_list:

```
write_list([]).
write_list([HeadTAIL]) :-
         write(" ", Head),
         write_list(Tail).
```

Write_list uses recursion to print out the new proposition after completing the translation. If the list is an empty list then all symbols have been printed. Otherwise, it prints the head of the list. It then recursively calls itself with the tail or remainder of the list.

The complete program follows:

```
/*  Translate          */

domains

  sym_list = symbol*


predicates

  eval(sym_list)
  parse(symbol, sym_list)
  repeat()
  translate()
  transform(sym_list, sym_list, symbol)
  write_list(sym_list)

clauses

  translate :-
         makewindow(1,1,7,"Proposition",1,1,20,60),
         repeat,
```

```
            write("\n\nEnter Proposition or q to quit.\n:   "),
            readln(Statement),
            parse(Statement, State_list),
            eval(State_list).

eval([q]).
eval(State_list) :-
            transform(State_list, Final_state, Reason),
            write( "\nFinal Proposition = " ),
            write_list(Final_state),
            write( "\nReduced By - ", Reason ),
            !, fail.


parse("", []).
parse(Statement, [Token|List]) :-
            fronttoken(Statement,Token,Remainder),
            parse(Remainder,List).

transform(["not", "(", "not", "X", ")"],
            ["X"], "Reduce Double Negation") :- !.

transform(["X", "=", "Y"],
            ["not", "X", "v", "Y"],
            "Eliminate Implication") :- !.

transform(["not", "(", "X", "&", "Y", ")"],
            ["not", "X", "v", "not", "Y"],
            "De Morgan's Theorem for And") :- !.

transform(["not", "(", "X", "v", "Y", ")"],
            ["not", "X", "&", "not", "Y"],
            "De Morgan's Theorem for Or") :- !.

transform(["X", "&", "Y", "v", "Z"],
            [ "(", "X", "v", "Z", ")", "&",
             "(", "Y", "v", "Z", ")"],
             "Distribution") :-!.

transform(["X", "v", "Y", "&", "Z"],
            ["(", "X", "v", "Z", ")", "&",
             "(", "X", "v", "Z", ")"],
             "Distribution") :- !.

transform(_, [], "") :-
            write("\nInitial proposition was not transformed."), !, fail.

write_list([]).
write_list([Head|TAIL]) :-
            write(" ", Head),
            write_list(Tail).

repeat.
repeat :- repeat.
```

To run Translate, enter:

```
translate
```

and a window is opened and the following statement is printed:

```
Enter Proposition or q to quit.
:    _
```

If a valid proposition is entered, such as "not(X & Y)," then the program will return the message:

```
Final Proposition = not X v not Y
Reduced By - De Morgan's Theorem for And
```

and the process continues.

Summary of Translate Program

This very simple program is designed to demonstrate how Turbo Prolog could be used with formal proposition logic. It also introduces some programming concepts that will be used later in the book. By adding a more sophisticated parsing technique, some recursive logic, and a more robust set of logic theorems and tautologies, Translate could perform more robust tasks. For example, it could be used as the basis of a theorem prover. This implementation has some limitations that can be corrected to enable processing of serious propositional logic. A primary limitation is that a variable has to be entered just as specified in the table, including the upper- and lowercase form.

The propositional calculus discussed in this section has its limitations. It can only determine whether a statement is true or false. What is missing is the ability to represent relationships between objects. An example will help illustrate:

```
Rover is a dog.
   or
Rover is a Saint Bernard.
```

These statements can not be formalized in propositional logic because the "is a" relationship does not exist. If you tried:

```
Rover_dog      and      Rover_Saint_Bernard
```

then each is defined as a separate object. There is no means of showing the relationship between them.

Predicate Calculus

Predicate calculus is an extension of propositional calculus. The same connectives are used; however, the logic statements support the representation of relationships between objects. In predicate calculus, predicates serve as the statements which define objects and the relationships that objects have with other objects. In computer terms, a predicate is a function that returns either a true or false value.

In this example, the three kingdoms of the natural world: animal, vegetable, and mineral are used to illustrate a classification problem. The predicates is_animal, is_vegetable, and is_mineral are used to express relationships about the objects as shown:

	is_animal	is_vegetable	is_mineral
house	False	False	True
dog	True	False	False
1	False	False	False
flower	False	True	False

In predicate calculus, some of these relationships are written:

```
is_animal( house )    -> False
is_animal( dog )      -> True
is_animal( 1 )        -> False
is_animal( flower )   -> False
```

In propositional calculus you must create a new statement for each function; however, in predicate calculus, a single function can be used with multiple objects. These examples use one argument for each predicate. Here is an example that uses two arguments:

```
equal( 213, 218 )    -> False
equal( 712, 712 )    -> True
```

Sometimes it is necessary to represent relations that are always valid. A statement such as, "The snow is always cold," can be expressed:

```
The snow is always cold    - - - > Vx snow( x )-->
cold( x ).
```

where Vx means "is always."

Another useful relation is "there exists." You can use this relation to express a statement such as, "There are cacti in Arizona." In predicate calculus notation, you can write this as:

```
There are cacti in Arizona - - - > Ex cacti( x ) &
located( x, AZ ).
```

Using Predicate Calculus

To help you understand how predicate calculus is used, a simple program is developed next. This example uses the following relationships:

a) The doctor is a time lord.   `time_lord(the_doctor )`

b) The doctor is a gallifren.   `gallifren( the_doctor )`

c) The doctor runs the tartus.   `tartus( the_doctor )`

d) The master is a villain.   `villain( the_master )`

e) The master is a time lord.   `time_lord( the_master )`

f) The master tried to destroy   `destroy( the_master, the_doctor.)`
    the doctor.

g) All time lords either like   `Vx time_lord( x ) -->`
    the doctor or they hate him.   `    likes( x, the_doctor ) v`
                                       `    hate( x, the_doctor )`

h) Everyone likes someone.   `VxEy likes( x, y )`

i) Gallifrens that are villains   `VxVy gallifren( x ) & villain( x ) &`
    only try to destroy time lords   `    destroy( x, y ) &`
    they do not like.   `    time_lord( y )`
                                       `    --> not likes( x, y )`

After looking over these relations, you might have some questions such as, does the master like the doctor? The answer to this question seems obvious because the master is a villain and he tried to destroy the doctor. On the other hand, there are no logic statements provided which prove this point. To illustrate this, a technique of backward reasoning is used. With backward reasoning, you start with a conclusion and work backward over the premises that lead to a conclusion.

To discover if the master does not like the doctor, you start with the conclusion:

```
not likes( master, doctor ).
```

This is the conclusion of rule (i). In its general form it is written as:

```
not likes( x, y )    where x = Master and y = Doctor
```

To determine if this conclusion is valid, you must work backwards and prove its premises:

```
time_lord( doctor )          -> True    -  predicate a)
destroy( master, doctor )-> True    - predicate f)
villain( master )            -> True    - predicate d)
gallifren( master )          -> Can't prove
```

Given the predicates that are available, you cannot prove that the master is a gallifren. The logic that defines the gallifren is missing. You can add the following definition, however:

```
j) All time lords are        Vx time_lord( x ) ->
   gallifren                   gallifren( x ).
```

Now you have the conclusion gallifren(master) which is true if the master is a time lord:

```
time_lord( master ) -> gallifren( master )
```

and because the master is a time lord then he must be a gallifren. Therefore, the master dislikes the doctor.

With Turbo Prolog, you can easily create a program to solve this problem. Here is the code:

```
/*  Predicate Logic Example */

predicates

    destroy(symbol, symbol)
    gallifren(symbol)
    hates(symbol, symbol)
    likes(symbol, symbol)
    not_likes(symbol, symbol)
    tartus(symbol)
    time_lord(symbol)
    villain(symbol)
```

(continued)

```
clauses
    gallifren( the_doctor ).

/*    gallifren( X ) :- time_lord( X ). */

    tartus( the_doctor ).

    villain( the_master ).

    destroy( the_master, the_doctor ).

    time_lord( the_doctor ).
    time_lord( the_master ).

    time_lord( X ) :-
                likes( X, the_doctor ).
    time_lord( X ) :-
                hates( X, the_doctor ).


    likes( X, Y ) :- time_lord( X ),
                     time_lord( Y ).

    not_likes( X, Y ) :-
        gallifren( X ),
        villain( X ),
        destroy( X, Y ),
        time_lord( Y ).

    hates( _, _ ).
```

The logic statements are written as clauses. Note that these clauses cannot be written in the same order as described in the problem because Turbo Prolog requires that similar clauses must be in the same order. Note that predicate (g) is converted into two statements because of the "or" function. Also, note that a dummy "hate" clause has been defined to represent the hate predicate used in rule (i). In Turbo Prolog it is necessary to use such dummy clauses because the compiled Prolog system expects that all clauses in a program must be defined.

When you run this program with the goal:

```
not_likes( the_master, the_doctor )
```

the system returns "False." Now, note the line of code:

```
gallifren( X ) :- time_lord( X ).
```

If you remove the comment from this line of code and run the program with the previous goal, the system returns "True."

Inference and Control Strategies

Now that you have seen how predicate logic is used to represent facts, relations, and reasoning, you are ready to move on and explore inference and control strategies. From the previous section, you should realize that predicate logic has its limitations for representing knowledge and performing reasoning. Fortunately, there are other approaches that overcome some of these limitations. One approach involves separating the information or knowledge about a problem from the reasoning mechanism. By customizing the knowledge and the reasoning mechanism to support a particular problem, a better program for simulating human reasoning can be constructed. This is an important characteristic of expert systems—programs that can perform like human experts. While traditional procedural programs combine knowledge and program control, expert systems separate knowledge and program control. The remainder of this chapter will focus in on the inference mechanism used in expert systems. Later, in Chapter 7, you will learn how to build complete expert systems.

The Inference Engine

The inference engine is the heart of an expert system. It simulates the reasoning processes that people use for problem solving activities. The inference engine performs two important tasks: the first is reasoning or inference and the other is control. The inference process is based on a system of formal logic similar to the predicate logic introduced earlier in this chapter. This process uses simple IF-THEN rules to manipulate facts. In this respect, an inference engine performs the function of a rule interpreter.

The control part, on the other hand, is responsible for determining the order in which rules are selected. Two of the more common control mechanisms are backward-chaining and forward-chaining. Backward-chaining is a simple technique of starting with a conclusion and working backward through sub-goals to determine if the conclusion is valid. This control strategy is actually built into Turbo Prolog. Forward-chaining, on the other hand, is the process of starting with known facts and working forward, trying to find a valid conclusion. Combinations of these two control strategies can be used to add more flexibility to an inference engine. Some "engines" even use meta-rules to define the control strategy and inferencing techniques used by the inference engine.

Using Backward-Chaining

As mentioned, backward-chaining is a goal-directed control strategy that begins with the final conclusion or goal. To reach this goal, certain conditions must be met. Some of these conditions may be facts while others are conclusions to other rules. The conclusions then become sub-goals which must be proven. The process continues to work backward, generating more sub-goals that must also be satisfied, until all the sub-goals have been met.

Here is an example of backward reasoning to help clarify how backward-chaining works. Assume you are living in New York City and you want to travel to a new town—Scottsdale, Arizona. If you first locate Scottsdale on a map, you will next have to find routes back to New York. Of course, you are now working backward from the direction you will be traveling. Once you are in familiar territory—the state of New York—you don't need the map. So your goal is to find a route connecting Scottsdale to New York.

Assume that the data is provided in the following form:

```
path(amarillo, texas, los_angeles, california).
path(amarillo, texas, scottsdale, arizona).
path(boston, massachusetts, st_louis, missouri).
path(st_louis, missouri, amarillo, texas).
```

The first two arguments are the city and state at the start of a path and the second two arguments are the city and state at the end of a path. A graphic representation of this data is shown in Figure 4.4. The state information will not be used but could be used if there were two cities of the same name in different states.

Find_route is the predicate which recursively checks the path data for a path from a start-point to an end-point.

```
find_route(Start, End):-
    path(Start, _, End,_),
    write("\nTravel from ", Start, " To ", End),nl.
```

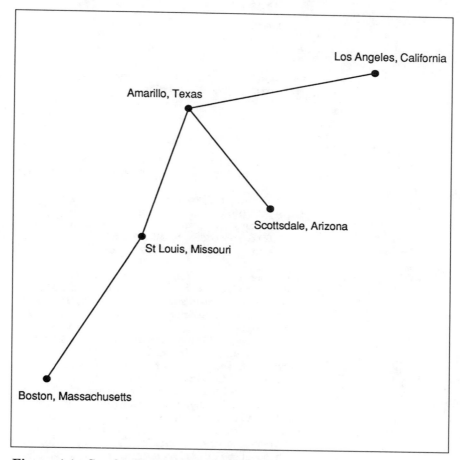

Figure 4.4   Graphic Representation of Routes

```
find_route(Start, End) :-
    path(Mid_Point, _, End, _),
    nl, /* Optional */
    find_route(Start, Mid_Point),
    write(" and from ", Mid_Point, " To ", End), nl.
```

The second find_route predicate uses the ending location to search the path table. This predicate looks for the beginning of a path that matches the given destination.

The complete program is:

```
/*    Backward Chaining   */

predicates
    path(symbol, symbol, symbol, symbol)
    find_route(symbol, symbol)

clauses
    find_route(Start, End):-

        path(Start, _, End,_),
        write("\nTravel from ", Start, " To ", End), nl.

    find_route(Start, End) :-
        path(Mid_Point, _, End, _),
        write("  Searching at ", Mid_Point, " To ", End), nl,
        find_route(Start, Mid_Point),
        write("  and from ", Mid_Point, " To ", End), nl.

    path(amarillo, texas, los_angeles, california).
    path(amarillo, texas, scottsdale, arizona).
    path(boston, massachusetts, st_louis, missouri).
    path(boston, massachusetts, chicago, illinois).
    path(chicago, illinois, denver, colorado).
    path(chicago, illinois, san_francisco, california).
    path(cleveland, ohio, chicago, illinois).
    path(cleveland, ohio, st_louis, missouri).
    path(miami, florida, memphis, tennesse).
    path(new_york_city, new_york, miami, florida).
    path(new_york_city, new_york, cleveland, ohio).
    path(portland, maine, boston, massachusetts).
    path(san_francisco, california, new_york_city, new_york).
    path(san_francisco, california, scottsdale, arizona).
    path(scottsdale, arizona, los_angeles, california).
    path(seattle, washington, san_francisco, california).
    path(st_louis, missouri, amarillo, texas).
    path(st_louis, missouri, denver, colorado).
```

You can test this program by specifying the goal:

```
find_route(new_york_city,  new_york,  scottsdale,
arizona).
```

The first time through, find_route looks for a path that begins
in New York City and terminates in Scottsdale. Since there
isn't such a path, the second version of find_route is called.
This predicate will determine that Amarillo is the beginning
of a path that ends in Scottsdale. Find_route then recursively
calls itself with New York City as the starting point and
Amarillo as the destination. This second call will attempt to

find a path that terminates in Amarillo. In other words, find_route is starting from Scottsdale and attempting to backtrack to New York City. Once a path is found that starts in New York City, then the first predicate is matched. The first find_route predicate terminates the recursion because the backtracking has reached the initial conditions. It then prints the starting and ending locations of the first leg of the trip. Now that this predicate is successful, it must unwind all of its recursive calls. As it does, each call prints the leg of the path that it matched. This is useful because dead-end paths may be checked but they are never printed—only the final and successful path is printed. The optional write statement included in find_route allows you to watch the paths that are actually checked.

You could improve this example by adding a rule for making selections. Currently, the program will return only the first path it finds and this may not be the shortest path. After all, you wouldn't want to travel from Boston to New York City via San Francisco. Try it. Also, since find_route only finds one solution, the order of the paths in the program are important. Finally, there is no protection from circular data. That is, cities with paths that eventually lead back to themselves.

Using Forward-Chaining

As you might expect, forward-chaining is the reverse of backward-chaining. This control strategy starts with known facts and works toward a conclusion. The previous program can easily be modified to perform forward-chaining. The path predicate is used again; however, some new entries have been added. Because there are paths from New York City, to Cleveland, to Chicago, to San Francisco, and finally back to New York City, a circular loop is formed. The backward-chaining example was not designed to handle this type of problem. This example of forward-chaining, however, is able to work around this problem.

You should now type in the following program:

```
/*   Forward-Chaining  Program */
   database

      record(symbol, symbol)
      route(symbol, symbol)
```

(continued)

```
predicates

    find_route(symbol, symbol)
    path(symbol, symbol, symbol, symbol)
    run(symbol, symbol)
    write_route(symbol, symbol)

clauses

    run(_, _) :-
        retract(_),
        fail.

    run(Start, End) :-
        find_route(Start, End), nl,
        write_route(Start, End), nl.

    find_route(Start, End) :-

        path(Start, _, End,_),
        write("\nSearching from ", Start, " To ", End),
        asserta(route(Start, End)).

    find_route(Start, End) :-
        path(Start, _, Mid_Point, _),
        not(record(Start,Mid_Point)),
        assertz(record(Start, Mid_Point)),
        write("\nSearching at ", Start, " To ", Mid_Point),
        find_route(Mid_Point, End),
        asserta(route(Start, Mid_point)).

    write_route(Start, End) :-
        route(Start, End),
        write("\n", Start, " To ", End).

    write_route(Start, End) :-
        route(Start, Mid_Point),
        write("\n", Start, " To ", Mid_Point),
        write_route(Mid_Point, End).

    path(amarillo, texas, los_angeles, california).
    path(amarillo, texas, scottsdale, arizona).
    path(boston, massachusetts, chicago, illinois).
    path(boston, massachusetts, st_louis, missouri).
    path(chicago, illinois, san_francisco, california).
    path(chicago, illinois, denver, colorado).
    path(cleveland, ohio, chicago, illinois).
    path(cleveland, ohio, st_louis, missouri).
    path(las_vegas,nevada, scottsdale, arizona).
    path(miami, florida, memphis, tennesse).
    path(new_york_city, new_york, miami, florida).
    path(new_york_city, new_york, cleveland, ohio).
```

```
path(portland, maine, boston, massachusetts).
path(san_francisco, california, portland, maine).
path(san_francisco, california, las_vegas, nevada).
path(san_francisco, california, new_york_city, new_york).
path(scottsdale, arizona, los_angeles, california).
path(seattle, washington, san_francisco, california).
path(st_louis, missouri, amarillo, texas).
path(st_louis, missouri, denver, colorado).
```

Run is the main clause in this example. The first run clause is used to initialize the database. It retracts information that may have been asserted during an earlier run. When the run predicate fails, the second predicate is called. It contains two main sub-goals. The first determines the route from start to finish. The second one is used to print the route in the correct order. Unlike the backtracking example, the information can not be printed as the recursion is unwound because the order of the return calls due to the recursion is the opposite of the order of the true path.

The recursive technique used by find_route is similar to the technique used in the backtracking example, except here the program looks for matches with the initial path argument instead of the final path argument. There are two major differences in the functions performed by this version of find_route. First, a marker called "record" is made of every path taken. This "marker" is implemented as a database clause. If an attempt is made to take a path a second time, the marker forces that pass through find_route to fail. If a new path is found that has not been used before, it is asserted to the database. This prevents the endless loop from occurring.

The second difference is that the route is not printed out as the recursion unfolds. This information is asserted into the database with the route clause. Thus, it will be ready to print in the correct order by the write_route clause. The write_route predicates are implemented in the same recursive style as the find_route predicate.

Forward-Chaining vs. Backward-Chaining

After working with these examples, you might still be wondering about which type of control strategy is more useful. To answer this, a number of factors must be considered. If you are solving a problem with significantly more goal states, then it is easier to use a forward-chaining strategy. On the other hand, backward-chaining strategies are better suited for problems that have more start states, and they are easier to develop in Turbo Prolog because the backtracking feature is built into the language. In the inference engine example presented next, the backward-chaining control strategy is used because of its simplicity.

Developing an Inference Engine

After exploring the fundamentals of an inference engine, you should be able to write one in Turbo Prolog. As you develop the inference engine, keep in mind that it is the central part of an expert system. To simplify the discussion about the "engine," the important tasks are identified. The following brief overview is followed by a more detailed explanation along with the code for a simple inference engine. A block diagram of the inference engine is shown in Figure 4.5.

The two main tasks of the inference engine are the scheduler and the rule interpreter. These are described as follows:

- The scheduler determines which facts, rules, and relationships should be used by selecting a control strategy such as forward-chaining and/or backward-chaining.

- The rule interpreter processes the rules selected by the scheduler. It matches up rules with the known facts and performs the actions specified by the rules. It also stores results for later use by the inference engine, or executes any actions that might be of interest.

In addition to the scheduler and the rule interpreter, these three other tasks are performed by the inference engine:

- The uncertainty processor helps handle facts and data that are not completely defined or whose certainty is not clear. This allows the inference engine to work with incomplete or unreliable data.

- The why processor explains to the user why a specific inference is made by the inference engine.

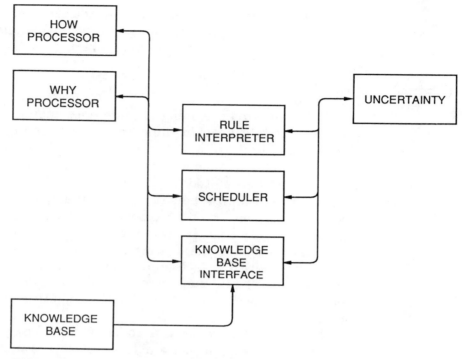

Figure 4.5   Components of an Inference Engine

- The how processor explains the facts, rules, and decision processes that were used by the inference engine to reach a final conclusion.

Finally, some type of interface is needed to allow the inference engine to gather the needed facts and rules in order to perform inferences. The facts and rules are stored in what is commonly called a knowledge base. For this example a simple set of rules and facts are grouped together in the knowledge base. The interface aids the communication process between the knowledge base and the inference engine. Here is the definition for the knowledge base interface:

- The knowledge base interface obtains facts and rules from the knowledge base as requested by the rule interpreter and scheduler.

In the next section you will first build the two main components of the inference engine—the scheduler and the rule interpreter. Of course, it will also be necessary to create a simple knowledge interface to test out the "engine." Next, you will learn how to modify the program to support uncertainty. Finally the why and how processors will be added.

Getting Started

While you are developing the inference engine in this section, you should keep in mind that these "engines" can be used for different types of applications. Classification and diagnostic applications, however, are among the most common types of problems suited for inference engines. These include problems from auto repair or medical diagnosis through insect classification. In these types of problems, the inference engines' primary objective is to reduce the number of possible solutions. It makes these decisions based on input data in conjunction with the facts and rules in the knowledge base. The inference engine that you are about to develop in this section can solve both types of problems—diagnostic and classification.

The diagnostic example used is that of fixing a broken computer. To perform such a task, there are a number of things which must be checked including software and peripherals. Peripherals, such as printers, are more likely to fail than anything else. Therefore, one possible reasoning process used by a computer repair person might be:

```
Computers have printers that fail
       Printer has ribbons that can jam or run out
               Resulting possibilities - Replace ribbon
            .
            .
       Printer has cables that become disconnected
       Printer has baud and parity switches that can be
       changed
       .
       .
       .
```

The goal here is to apply the inference process to focus in on a possible solution to a specific problem. In the inference engine example, you will discover how this process can be simulated. A classification example is also presented in the next section to help you understand how the inference engine operates.

Writing the Engine

The core of the inference engine, including the scheduler, the rule interpreter, and the knowledge interface, is developed first. The scheduler is implemented using a backward-chaining control strategy:

```
scheduler(Major, Minor) :-
        k_base_interface(Major, Minor).

scheduler(Major, Subset) :-
        k_base_interface(Major, Minor),
        scheduler(Minor, Subset).
```

As shown, the scheduler accesses the knowledge interface with the k_base_interface clause. K_base_interface makes direct calls to the knowledge base to obtain information for the scheduler. This clause is explained in more detail in a following section.

Closely tied with the scheduler is the rule interpreter. The code for this part of the system consists of the following:

```
rule_interpreter(Result, Reason) :-
        possible_solutions(Result, Reason).

rule_interpreter(Result, Reason) :-
        scheduler(Result, Search),
        possible_solutions(Search, Reason).
```

Here the rule interpreter uses the scheduler to follow the relationships within the knowledge base. Once a decision is made by the scheduler, the resulting facts are obtained from the knowledge base. These facts are obtained by a call to the possible_solutions clause which obtains information from the knowledge base. As the name of the clause implies, this clause returns "a possible solution" for a diagnostic or classification problem.

At this point some discussion about the knowledge base is needed. In this example, a modular approach is used to separate the knowledge base from the rest of the inference engine via the k_base_interface clause:

```
k_base_interface(Field1, Field2) :-
        k_base_facts(Field1, Field2).
```

This clause accesses the knowledge base directly with k_base_facts. The knowledge base used is very simple. It consists of some basic facts about computers and constellations— two very unrelated subjects. Here is the knowledge base which is stored as the file "know_bas.pro":

```
predicates                                    /* simple knowledge base */
                                              /* know_bas.pro    */
    k_base_facts(symbol,symbol)
    possible_solutions(symbol,symbol)

clauses

    k_base_facts(computer,printer).
    k_base_facts(printer,ribbon).
    k_base_facts(printer,cable).

    k_base_facts(constellations, northern_hem).
    k_base_facts(northern_hem, spring).
    k_base_facts(northern_hem, summer).
    k_base_facts(spring, stars_7).
    k_base_facts(summer, stars_16).

    possible_solutions(ribbon,ribbon_empty).
    possible_solutions(cable,disconnected_cable).
    possible_solutions(stars_7, big_dipper).
    possible_solutions(stars_16, scorpius).
```

This knowledge base is represented as a static file; although typically the knowledge base is represented as a dynamic database and stored as a consult file. Note that there are two completely unrelated sets of relations in the knowledge base. The first set of facts refer to the relationships that exist between a computer and a printer. The following example, k_base_facts(computer, printer), can be interpreted as stating "the computer has a printer." This allows you to test the diagnostic as well as classification capability of the inference engine. The second set of facts refer to a set of relationships for classifying a constellation.

If the knowledge base were more complicated or if it ever changes, having the knowledge base interface localized in a few clauses would reduce the effect those changes have on other parts of the inference engine. The concept of the knowledge base will be covered in greater detail in Chapter 6.

Finally, the core of the inference engine can be put together. You should enter the following code now:

```
include "know_bas.pro"          /*  The knowledge base is a separate file
                                    that is included here.  */
predicates

    k_base_interface(symbol,symbol)
    rule_interpreter(symbol,symbol)
    scheduler(symbol,symbol)

clauses

    k_base_interface(Field1, Field2) :-
        k_base_facts(Field1, Field2).

    rule_interpreter(Result, Reason) :-
        possible_solutions(Result, Reason).

    rule_interpreter(Result,Reason) :-
        scheduler(Result, Search),
        possible_solutions(Search, Reason).

    scheduler(Major, Minor) :-
        k_base_interface(Major, Minor).

    scheduler(Major, Subset) :-
        k_base_interface(Major, Minor),
        scheduler(Minor, Subset).
```

Now that the first version of the interpreter and scheduler
are complete, you can test them out by specifying some goals.
If you type in:

```
scheduler(computer, X).
```

thus requesting the scheduler to tell you about all of the existing relationships between the term "computer" and the other
facts in the knowledge base, the system will respond with:

```
X = printer
X = ribbon
X = cable
```

The first response, "X = computer," should be obvious from
the facts stored in the knowledge base. The second response,
"X = ribbon," was discovered by the scheduler because of the
two facts in the knowledge base:

```
k_base_facts(computer, printer).
k_base_facts(printer, ribbon).
```

These facts define two relationships: "the computer has a printer" and "the printer has a ribbon." Therefore, the scheduler infers that some type of relationship exists between a computer and a ribbon. The third response, "X = cable," was also discovered by the scheduler in the same manner as the previous response. You should go over this logic to make sure you understand exactly what the scheduler is doing.

Now that you have seen how the scheduler works, you might want to try out the rule interpreter. If you enter a goal such as:

```
rule_interpreter(computer, X)
```

you will obtain the responses:

```
X = ribbon_empty
X = disconnected_cable
```

These two responses indicate the two possible solutions or outcomes associated with the term "computer." Remember that this inference engine can perform diagnostic-like tasks, thus you could interpret these responses as examples of what might be wrong with the computer.

Repeat the test of the rule interpreter with the first argument equal to "constellations" to try out the constellations part of the knowledge base.

Adding the Test Driver

To improve the inference engine, a test driver can be added. This test driver will allow you to exercise the full capabilities of the inference engine. This program now consists of two parts: a re-packaged inference engine and the core of the test driver. The inference engine is now written as:

```
inference(Result)  :-
        rule_interpreter(Result, Reason),
        ask_user(confirmed(Result, Reason)),
        add_new(Result, Reason).

ask_user(Clause)  :-
        write("\n", Clause, " y/n"),
        readchar(Answer),
        Answer = 'y',
        assertz(Clause).
```

```
add_new(Result, Reason) :
      asserta(new_result(Result, Reason)).
```

This clause acts as the highest level clause of the engine; it makes the calls to the other functions. Here, two new clauses have been added, ask_user and add_new. Ask_user queries you to see if the relationship found by the rule interpreter is a valid response. If you answer "yes," then the clause is asserted as a verified solution. Add_new, the other clause added, asserts the current solution and reason to the database.

The code for the entire program is shown here:

```
/* The Complete Inference Engine */

include "know_bas.pro"            /* example knowledge base */

database

    confirmed(symbol,symbol)
    new_result(symbol,symbol)
    result_action(symbol,symbol)

predicates

    init_data()
    proc_user(char)
    print(char)
    repeat()
    test_inference()
    k_base_interface(symbol, symbol)
    rule_interpreter(symbol, symbol)
    scheduler(symbol, symbol)
    inference(symbol)
    add_new(symbol, symbol)
    ask_user(dbasedom)


clauses

    test_inference() :-
        makewindow( 1, 1, 7, "Inference Engine", 1, 1, 20, 60 ),
        repeat(),
        write( " \n\n* * * * * * * * * * * * * * * *\nTest Program" ),
        write( "\nh - Help, i - initialize," ),
        write( "\np - Print, q - Quit, r - Run" ),
        write( "\nWhat type of entry (h/i/p/q/r) ?  " ),
        readchar( Choice ),
        proc_user( Choice ).
```

(continued)

```
proc_user( 'q' ).

proc_user( 'r' ) :-
     write( "\nWhat is your query?  "),
     readln( Query ),
     inference( Query ),
     fail.

proc_user( 'p' ) :-
     write( "\n* * * * * * * * * * * *\nCurrent Information." ),
     write( "\nc - confirmed options, t - how list, " ),
     write( "\nPrint what type of information (c/t) ?  "),
     readchar( Choice ),
     print( Choice ).

proc_user( 'i' ) :-
     write( "\nReset - Clear out all Information (y/n)." ),
     readln( Response ),
     Response = y,
     init_data(),
     fail.

init_data() :-
     retract(confirmed(_, _)),
     retract(new_result(_, _)).

print('c') :- confirmed(Result, Reason),
     write( "\nConfirmed Reasons - ", Result, ", ", Reason, "  "),
     fail.

print('t') :- new_result(Result, Reason),
     write("\nNew Results - ", Result, ", ", Reason, "  "),
     fail.


/*******************************************************************/
/*                  Inference Engine                             */


k_base_interface(Field1, Field2) :-
     k_base_facts(Field1, Field2).

rule_interpreter(Result, Reason) :-
     possible_solutions(Result, Reason).

rule_interpreter(Result,Reason) :-
     scheduler(Result, Search),
     possible_solutions(Search, Reason).

scheduler(Major, Minor) :-
     k_base_interface(Major, Minor).
```

```
scheduler(Major, Subset) :-
      k_base_interface(Major, Minor),
      scheduler(Minor, Subset).

inference(Result) :-
      rule_interpreter(Result, Reason),
      ask_user(confirmed(Result, Reason)),
      add_new(Result, Reason).

ask_user(Clause) :-
      write("\n", Clause, " y/n"),
      readchar(Answer),
      Answer = 'y',
      assertz(Clause).

add_new(Result, Reason) :
      asserta(new_result(Result, Reason)).
```

The clauses, test_inference, proc_user, init_data, and print, make up the test driver. The test_inference clauses lists the valid options for using this program and then executes the selected option. The four options available are initialize, print, quit, and run. Once an option is selected, the appropriate proc_user clause is called. Initialize resets the asserted data from a previous run. The print option displays the data that is asserted. The quit option terminates the program and the run option starts the inference engine. To avoid confusion and to simplify re-initialization, the dynamic data generated by the asserts (confirmed, new_result, result_action) is separated from the known or expert data which is in "know_bas.pro."

To test the inference engine, type in the following goal:

```
test_inference.
```

When the program starts, you can request a query by entering "r." At this point, you will receive the message:

```
What is your query?
```

Try out the query "computer," and you will activate the inference engine.

Uncertainty

The inferencing technique used in the example doesn't tell you anything about the level of confidence or certainty in the final conclusions. The degree of accuracy or certainty of the facts and rules are completely ignored. This is not very realistic because the world is not so "black or white"—most decisions that you make are often not completely accurate. The doctor is never one hundred percent certain what is ailing his or her patient and the programmer is never completely sure that his or her program will run correctly the first time. Fortunately, techniques are available for measuring the uncertainty in the results of an inference engine. One such technique is called uncertainty processing. There are a number of approaches to handling this uncertainty. In this section, one of these approaches, the uncertainty factor, is presented.

The uncertainty factor is simply a weight factor that can be added separately to each rule, fact, or user supplied data item. This weight factor serves as an estimate of how accurate, or inaccurate, the fact or rule is. Weather forecasting provides a good illustration of a science that routinely uses such a factor. In this case, the weight factor is a probability with a value from 0 to 100 percent. For example, if you ask the question:

```
Is it going to rain this afternoon?
```

A weather forecaster might answer by using the rule:

```
The probability of afternoon rain is the average
of the probabilities of the temperature being over
90 degrees, and the sky being partly cloudy, and
the monsoon weather occurring.
```

The forecaster checks the weather instruments and determines:

```
There is a 95% probability that the temperature will
    be greater than 90 degrees.
There is a 85% probability that the sky will be
    partly cloudy.
There is a 100% probability that this is the summer
    monsoon season.
```

The forecaster therefore concludes that there is a 93% chance of afternoon precipitation because the rule states the total probability is the average of the probabilities of the three factors. Usually more elaborate methods including probability theories, formal uncertainty theories, and mathematical algorithms are used to perform such a calculation. In addition, certainty factors are often calculated as weight factors which are based on specific aspects of the problem being solved. Often, they are arbitrarily set by the designer of the system and then modified as necessary to provide answers that are consistent with the actual facts. This is the case for the inference engine that is being built in this section.

For this inference engine to be completely useful, it needs rules for detecting faults by their partial characteristics. That is, there may be only partial evidence for a particular fault. This could be due to a partial failure or to multiple failures covering up some of the symptoms. The certainty can be interpreted as a weight factor to the degree of which the characteristic or symptom is responsible for the fault. This also provides a nice, although not very accurate, level of confidence in the final decision.

The ability to handle uncertainty is provided by adding an extra argument to each of the rules, assertions, and clauses. In addition, a clause is added that processes the uncertainty factors per the chosen method, which in this case is just doing an average. When you are asked for supplemental information, in the form of the confirmations, you are also asked how certain you are of your answer. Therefore, the uncertainty processor uses your level of uncertainty. The uncertainty is implemented as an integer indicating 0 to 100 percent certainty.

The first change to the program occurs in the knowledge base. Note the changes:

```
/*  Changes in the knowledge base for uncertainty */


    k_base_facts(computer,printer,80).
    k_base_facts(printer,ribbon,90).
    k_base_facts(printer,cable,20).

    k_base_facts(constellations, northern_hem,40).
    k_base_facts(northern_hem, spring,95).
    k_base_facts(northern_hem, summer,95).
    k_base_facts(spring, stars_7,50).
    k_base_facts(summer, stars_16,30).

    possible_solutions(ribbon,ribbon_empty,90).
    possible_solutions(cable,disconnected_cable,30).
    possible_solutions(stars_7, big_dipper,70).
    possible_solutions(stars_16, scorpius,50).
```

The uncertainty factors added to the computer example indicate the probability that a computer has a printer (80%) or that a printer has a ribbon (90%) or cable (20%).

The second set of changes occur in the core of the rule interpreter:

```
/* changes in the core of the rule interpreter for uncertainty */


k_base_interface(Field1, Field2, Certainty) :-
        k_base_facts(Field1, Field2, Certainty).

scheduler(Major, Minor, Certainty) :-
        k_base_interface(Major, Minor, Certainty).
scheduler(Major, Subset, Certainty) :-
        k_base_interface(Major, Minor, Certainty_1),
        scheduler(Minor, Subset, Certainty_2),
        uncertainty(Certainty_1, Certainty_2, Certainty).

rule_interpreter(Result, Reason, Certainty) :-
        possible_solutions(Result, Reason, Certainty).

rule_interpreter(Result,Reason, Certainty) :-
        scheduler(Result, Search, Certainty_1),
        possible_solutions(Search, Reason, Certainty_2),
        uncertainty(Certainty_1, Certainty_2, Certainty).

uncertainty(Certain_1, Certain_2, Certainty) :-
        Certainty = (Certain_1 + Certain_2) / 2.
```

The uncertainty only needs to be processed where there is doubt about the quality or reliability of the information or knowledge base. For example, if it is known that all computers have printers, and all printers have ribbons, etc. then this uncertainty could be removed because there is no uncertainty.

The core of the inference engine is now:

```
/* changes in the core of the inference engine for uncertainty */


inference(Result) :-
        rule_interpreter(Result, Reason, Certainty_1),
        ask_user(Result, Reason, Certainty_2),
        uncertainty(Certainty_1,Certainty_2,Certainty),
        add_new(Result, Reason, Certainty).

ask_user(Result, Reason, Certainty) :-
        write("\nDoes ", Reason, " follow from ", Result, " (y/n)?"),
        readchar(Answer),
```

```
                    Answer = 'y',
                    write( "\nCertainty? "),
                    readint(Certainty),
                    assertz(confirmed(Result,Reason,Certainty)).

            add_new(Result, Reason, Certainty) :-
                    asserta(new_result(Result, Reason, Certainty)).
```

And the changes to the test driver are the following:

```
/* changes to the test driver */

    init_data() :-
         retract(confirmed(_, _, _)),
         retract(new_result(_, _, _)).

    print('c') :- confirmed(Result, Reason, Certainty),
         write( "\nConfirmed Reasons - ", Result, ", ", Reason, ", ",
                    Certainty),
         fail.

    print('t') :- new_result(Result, Reason, Certainty),
         write("\nNew Results - ", Result, ", ", Reason, ", ", Certainty),
         fail.
```

At this point, you should run the test driver as shown earlier. This time it will ask for an uncertainty value, such as 80, after asking for confirmation that the suggested fault is a possibility. Here is an example you should try out. First specify the goal:

```
    test_inference
```

and then select the "r" option. Next, type in the response "computer." You should continue with the following responses:

```
    y
    80
    n
    p
    t
```

The resulting print-out contains a trace of the inferencing process. The bottom five entries are the entries we are interested in:

```
    Tag - inferencing, computer, ribbon_empty, 84
    Tag - interpreter, computer, ribbon_empty, 88
    Tag - scheduler, printer, ribbon, 85
```

```
Tag - scheduler, printer, ribbon, 90
Tag - scheduler, printer, ribbon, 80
```

As this trace is stored as a first-in-last-out queue, the first trace value is at the bottom of the print-out. The bottom line represents the uncertainty factor for the computer having a printer (80). The next one is the uncertainty factor for the printer having a ribbon (90). Finally, the combined uncertainty, which is calculated by the uncertainty clause, is the uncertainty that the computer has a printer and that the printer has a ribbon (85). This is shown in the third line up from the bottom. Next, the uncertainty for the computer problem is the printer ribbon is (90). This came straight from the "possible_solutions" facts in the knowledge base. This is combined with the current 85 uncertainty giving 87.5 or rounded up to 88, which is in the fourth line up. Now, the uncertainty you added of 80 is combined with the 88 to give the final uncertainty of 84, which is the inferencing conclusion for the computer problem—an empty ribbon. Note that the final uncertainty is not greater than the highest uncertainty which was 90. Any facts that are very uncertain will tend to bring the certainty down.

The Why and How Processors

Another improvement that can be made to the inference engine is adding the why and how processors. The why processor offers an explanation for why a given question is asked and the how processor offers an explanation for how a decision was reached. In order to support these features, the inference engine must know the context by which the request for information was generated. One technique for achieving this is to pass a description of the context as an extra argument to each rule, similar to the way it was done for the uncertainty.

To support the why processor the knowledge base must be changed:

```
/* knowledge base chage to support why processor */

domains

    possible_solutions(symbol,symbol,integer,string)
```

```
clauses
    possible_solutions(ribbon,ribbon_empty,90,
        "The printer ribbon is often the cause for printer problems.").
    possible_solutions(cable,disconnected_cable,30,
        "The printer cable may be disconnected at computer or printer.").
    possible_solutions(stars_7, big_dipper,20,
        "Seven major star could be the big dipper.").
    possible_solutions(stars_16, scorpius,50,
        "Sixteen major stars could be the constellation scorpius.").
```

These changes must be made to the scheduler:

```
/* changes must be made to the scheduler */

    scheduler(Major, Minor, Certainty) :-
        k_base_interface(Major, Minor, Certainty),
        add_new(scheduler, Major, Minor, Certainty).

    scheduler(Major, Subset, Certainty) :-
        k_base_interface(Major, Minor, Certainty_1),
        scheduler(Minor, Subset, Certainty_2),
        uncertainty(Certainty_1, Certainty_2, Certainty),
        add_new(scheduler, Minor, Subset, Certainty).

    rule_interpreter(Result, Reason, Certainty) :-
        possible_solutions(Result, Reason, Certainty, _),
        add_new(interpreter, Result, Reason, Certainty).

    rule_interpreter(Result,Reason, Certainty) :-
        scheduler(Result, Search, Certainty_1),
        possible_solutions(Search, Reason, Certainty_2, _),
        uncertainty(Certainty_1, Certainty_2, Certainty),
        add_new(interpreter, Result, Reason, Certainty).
```

The inference engine core now is written:

```
/* the inference engine core for the why processor */


    inference(Result) :-
        rule_interpreter(Result, Reason, Certainty_1),
        ask_user(Result, Reason, Certainty_2),
        uncertainty(Certainty_1,Certainty_2,Certainty),
        add_new(inferencing, Result, Reason, Certainty).

    ask_user(Result, Reason, Certainty) :-
        write("\nDoes ", Reason, " follow from ", Result, " (y/n/?)?"),
        readchar(Answer),
        ask_user_1(Answer,Result, Reason, Certainty).
```

(continued)

```
ask_user_1(Answer, Result, Reason, Certainty) :-
     Answer = 'y',
     write( "\nCertainty? "),
     readint(Certainty),
     assertz(confirmed(Result,Reason,Certainty)).

ask_user_1(Answer, Result, Reason, Certainty) :-
     Answer = '?',
     possible_solutions(_, Reason, _, Why),
     write("\nWhy - ", Why ),
     ask_user(Result, Reason, Certainty).

add_new(Tag, Result, Reason, Certainty) :-
     asserta(new_result(Tag, Result, Reason, Certainty)).
```

And the new test driver is:

```
/* the new test driver for the why processor */


init_data() :-
     retract(confirmed(_, _, _)),
     retract(new_result(_, _, _, _)).

print('t') :- new_result(Tag, Result, Reason, Certainty),
     write("\nTag - ", ", Result, ", ", Reason, ", ", Certainty),
     fail.
```

Explanation of the Why and How Processors

Consider the why processor first. If you want to know why you are being asked to verify a fact that the inference engine produces then select this option. The why processor then displays the reason obtained from the knowledge base. That is, only the reason for choosing the "possible_solutions" is explained when you ask the system. To ask the system why it produces a given result, you simply enter "?" when the program queries you for a confirmation.

The following improvements could be added to the sample inference engine to improve the why capability. Additional arguments could be added to all the rules, facts, and the clauses that process them. This information could be displayed as part of the output for a why request. A partial explanation of the logic used to reach a question could also be included. One method for doing this is to save the reason for each accepted fact or rule in a list. The why command could then return the last reason added to the list. When the list is empty, a special message could be displayed.

The how processor adds a tag to the "add_new" clause so that the name of the clause being processed can be saved along with the arguments. The "add_new" clause is added to the end of clauses so that if they are successful, the pertinent information is saved. The trace can be seen by using the "p" command and selecting the trace option.

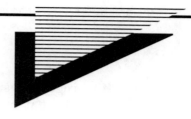

CHAPTER 5

Natural Language Processing

The real problem with today's computers is that they don't understand us when we use language the way we are used to.

from "The Cognitive Computer."
—Roger Schank

Developing a computer system that can understand a natural language such as English is not a simple task. AI researchers have been working at the many problems related to the creation of natural language processing programs since the early 1950s. Computers capable of understanding natural languages would provide us with enormous benefits. After all, if a computer could understand sentences that were typed in or spoken, most of us would find computers extremely easy to use. Natural language processing interfaces would eliminate the need to become computer literate. You also would not have to learn a computer language to program your computer because you could give the computer instructions in your own native language. For example, if you wanted to sort all of the files stored in a given directory, you might type in:

```
Sort all of the files in the Turbo Prolog directory.
```

and the program would understand what you wanted it to accomplish. If for some reason it could not carry out your command, it might respond back with a question such as:

```
Where is the Turbo Prolog directory?
```

If a program responded in such a manner, you would probably think that it possessed some type of intelligence. Of course, any program which could communicate like this would have to contain knowledge of the English language and of the topic or domain about which it is being questioned.

Even though it might seem that creating a computer program to understand English is an enormously difficult task, many successful natural language interface programs have been written in the past. These programs, however, usually can understand only a limited subset of English. By reducing the complexities to a more manageable size, AI researchers have been able to accomplish greater goals. But as you will also discover in this chapter, the real challenge which takes place when you attempt to develop a natural language processing system is trying to understand the ways in which people use language.

What Is a Natural Language?

You might think that this is a ridiculous question to ask, but more than likely you take your native language for granted because you first learned it through a natural process. In fact, most things that are learned through a natural process are taken for granted. Computers, however, are wonderful devices for encouraging us to think differently and question the natural ways of learning. For example, as soon as you sit down at your computer and type in the sentence:

```
How many files do I have on drive c?
```

and the computer responds:

```
Bad command or file name
```

you quickly discover that a natural language such as English is not so "natural" at least as far as the computer is concerned. When you learned English, you listened and spoke with humans rather than machines and you developed the techniques for communication by imitating other people.

Most often, the learning of a language is done at an early age in a very natural setting. You learned to associate sounds and phrases with events and physical objects found in the world. You also learned very quickly how to use language to express your emotions. The process of communication and language development is not very well defined, however. Because of this, it is very difficult to build computer models of natural languages. The languages that people use to communicate with each other are constantly growing and changing.

Natural languages are very different from the languages that computers are programmed in. Computer languages are considered to be formal or artificial languages. They have been developed by people so that communication with computers is possible. When you present your computer with such a statement:

```
type program.pro
```

you are actually using words and phrases of a language that has been carefully defined by a set of formal rules. Each statement in such a formal language can have only one meaning. The computer always responds to a formal statement in exactly the same manner. In this case, the computer would display the file "program.pro" on the screen because the command "type" has only one meaning as far as the computer is concerned. Of course, this is not true about the way people use natural languages. A sentence such as:

```
John wants to get a mouse.
```

would be difficult to understand unless you were fully aware of the context of the statement. The word "mouse" is ambiguous since it is not clear from this sentence that John wants a live mouse for a pet or that he wants a pointing device for his computer.

When you write statements in Turbo Prolog, you are also using a type of formal language. As an example, if you were to write a statement in Turbo Prolog, such as:

```
understands(mary, computers).
```

the statement would be interpreted by the Turbo Prolog environment as a fact consisting of the two terms "mary" and "computers." A one-to-one correspondence exists between every statement that you could write and an action that the computer must perform. In a natural language, such as English, this is not the case. So the real hurdle in developing natural language processing systems is to learn how to bridge the gap between the formal or artificial languages of the computer and the natural languages used by people. (See Figure 5.1.)

To simplify our discussion about natural languages in the rest of this chapter, it might be helpful for us to use our native English to represent natural languages.

Ingredients for Understanding Language

In order for anyone to be able to understand sentences in English, there are at least two important aspects that must be considered. First, you must have a good working knowledge of the rules or grammar of the language. The grammar rules define the ways in which words or phrases can be combined to create sentences. If you came across the following sentence:

```
The dogs wild were park children in chasing the.
```

You probably would agree that this sentence is confusing. It seems likely that whoever wrote it did not follow the correct rules of grammar. But if you applied some of the basic rules of good grammar, you could easily fix the sentence and come up with a new version that might be:

```
The wild dogs were chasing children in the park.
```

Now the sentence is understandable because it follows a convention you are probably familiar with. The sentence contains a noun phrase: *The wild dogs*, and a verb phrase: *were chasing*

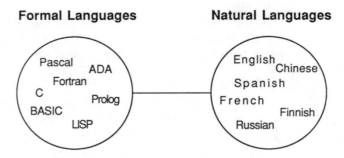

Figure 5.1   The Domain of Formal and Natural Languages

children in the park. One very popular and useful technique for representing such a sentence would be a grammar tree as shown in Figure 5.2.

The tree represents the syntax or structure of the sentence. It tells you how each of the components of the sentence are related to each other. These types of trees, commonly called parse trees, are very useful structures for representing different types of both natural and formal languages. The process of taking a sentence and breaking it up into its structural components is called syntactic analysis or parsing. You may have been taught how to do this in English courses.

Unfortunately, the syntactic analysis will tell you only half of the story. In order to really understand language, you must also have a good working knowledge of the meanings of words and an understanding about the context they are being used in. If you opened up an advanced book on physics and encountered this sentence:

```
The morphogenetic fields of morphic units influ-
ence morphogenesis by acting upon the morphogen-
etic fields of their constituent parts.
```

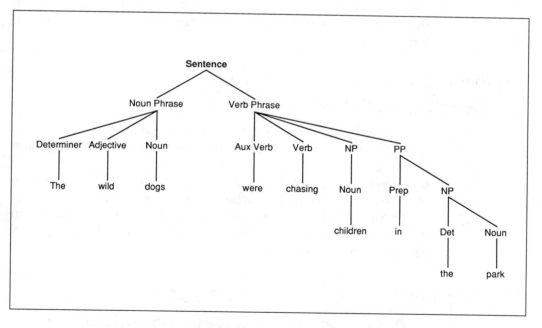

Figure 5.2   Representing a Sentence with a Grammar Tree

You would probably be completely confused unless you already had some experience with the subject matter. The sentence is constructed according to familiar grammar rules; however, the words used in the sentence are not part of a vocabulary you are probably familiar with. This illustrates the fact that you cannot understand the meaning of a sentence by looking only at its structure. If you wanted to investigate this point a little further, you could construct sentences such as:

```
The file cabinet sang to the housekeeper.
My cousin catches fish with a hammer.

If you water your computer every day and give it
plenty of sunlight, it will grow.
```

But none of these sentences make much sense, even though they are grammatically correct. Obviously, file cabinets cannot sing, people do not generally go fishing with hammers, and computers do not like or need water. If you really wanted to use language correctly you would have to consider the meaning or what is called the semantics of the words and phrases that you were using. This process of trying to work out the meaning of a sentence is called semantic analysis. Needless to say, this aspect is the most difficult to program into a computer because of the many ambiguities of natural languages.

Exploring Natural Language Processing Techniques

Many techniques for processing natural languages have been developed by AI researchers over the past thirty years. Some of the techniques are complex, and it would be difficult to present them in this chapter. Nonetheless, it is possible to write some programs in Turbo Prolog to perform simple analysis on basic English sentences. In the following sections, you will learn how to apply some of the useful techniques for processing English sentences.

The Pattern Matching Approach

One simplistic way of approaching the problem of processing English sentences is to use pattern matching techniques.

This approach makes use of patterns or key words which are stored as templates and matched against input sentences. For example, assume you have written a database program and you want to be able to accept and understand sentences such as:

```
Which employees worked overtime last week?
```

You might first realize that this sentence is a question because it ends with a "?". Therefore, if you wanted your database program to determine if the user was asking a question, you could have it scan the input sentence for a "?". From a programming standpoint, this task is easy to do. In fact you could simply use one of the tools developed in Chapter 3, such as the strcfind clause which searches for a character in a string. The operation can be performed with the call:

```
strcfind(Input, '?', Pos).
```

If strcfind locates the "?" you know that your sentence is a question.

The basic technique behind this approach is to scan the sentence for key words or phrases which are important and ignore the other words. If no matches are found then the sentence is not understood.

Even though the pattern matching approach to processing English sentences is very simple and limited, it can sometimes prove to be useful. Since this technique does not make use of grammar rules, it is often possible to understand sentences which are ungrammatical. For example, if you typed in a sentence such as:

```
Where are the all of Prolog files on drive A?
```

a good pattern matching program could understand what you are asking by ignoring the ungrammatical structure of the sentence and words like are, the, and of.

Using Transition Networks

The pattern matching technique does not tell us anything about the structure or syntax of sentences. The structural aspects are simply ignored by the pattern matcher. Unfortunately, this approach has limitations for practical applications and it does not represent very well the way that people use and understand language. To analyze the structural aspects of language, a better technique is needed. One useful system developed by AI researchers is called the transition network.

The transition network provides a good model for representing the grammatical structure of languages. Of course, there are many types of transition networks that have been developed by linguists and AI researchers. In this chapter, two of the fundamental transition networks, the recursive transition network and the augmented transition network, are presented. But before investigating how these particular transition networks operate, the general principles behind transition networks will be presented.

A transition network is actually a representational device which uses mathematical notations from graph theory to represent the structures of language. Transition networks have been used successfully to represent both natural and formal languages. In its simplest form, the transition network functions as a simple state machine. State machines are powerful devices which have often been used to represent the logical flow of control in digital computers. They can be constructed as a type of graph called the directed graph. An example of a simple state machine is shown in Figure 5.3. This form of transition network is called the state transition network. The circles with the labels, S0, S1, S2, and S3 are called nodes and they represent the various states. The labels A, B, C, and D represent the transitions. The states with the double circles, S2 and S3, are called terminal states or nodes and the initial or start state is represented by the state S0. To travel through this network, you simply start at the initial state, S0 and on encountering transition A, you move to state S1. Once you move to S1, you can either go to S3 or S2. Of course, this depends upon which transition you use. In this case, transition B will take you to state S3 and transition D will take you to S2. After you get to state S2, you are done because this state is a terminal state. The goal of using a transition network is to start at the initial state and move to a terminal state. The important point to keep in mind is that the transitions are responsible for directing the movement through the network. At any state in the network, a node can be represented as:

```
node (S0, A, S1)
```

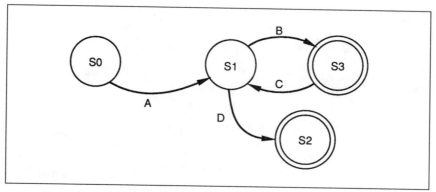

Figure 5.3   A Simple State Machine

where the first parameter, S0, represents the current state; the second parameter, A, represents the transition; and the last, S1, represents the state you will end up in after taking the transition.

Reading a transition network is a lot like reading a road map. You can think of the transition states as cities and the transitions themselves as major highways. Every city has a road which goes to one or more cities and you travel around by moving from city to city until you get to your final destination. Keep in mind, however, that transition networks can have more than one final state even though they always have only one initial state.

You might now be wondering: what do transition networks have to do with processing natural languages? Well, to get a better idea of how transition networks can be used, let us first come up with a simple set of grammar rules for a language. These rules are:

```
[1] Sentence      = Noun Phrase + Verb Phrase
[2] Noun Phrase   = Article + Noun
[3] Noun Phrase   = Noun
[4] Verb Phrase   = Verb + Noun Phrase2
[5] Noun Phrase2  = Article + Noun
[6] Noun Phrase2  = Article + Adjective + Noun
```

A parse tree representation for these rules is shown in Figure 5.4. To get a better understanding of how these rules work, let us look at them closely. Rule 1 tells us that a sentence consists of a noun phrase followed by a verb phrase. The noun phrase

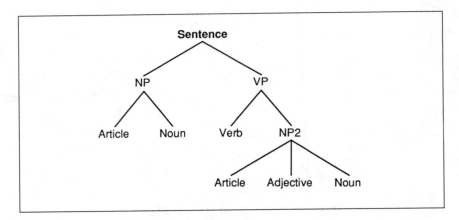

Figure 5.4   Tree Representation of Grammar Rules

can be either an article followed by a noun or just a noun. The verb phrase consists of a verb followed by a noun phrase which is slightly different than the first noun phrase. This noun phrase could consist of either an article followed by a noun or an article followed by an adjective and then a noun. With these simple rules, you can create meaningful English sentences provided you know what articles, adjectives, verbs, and nouns are. These elements were not defined in our rules, however, assume you are given the following words to work with:

Articles	Adjectives	Nouns	Verbs
the	fat	dog	chased
a	lazy	cat	wants
an	red	apple	likes
	crazy	John	
		Mary	

Combining the rules with our word definitions, sentences including:

```
The dog chased the fat cat.
          or
John wants the red apple.
```

can be created easily. And now that our grammar rules have been constructed, a simple state transition network can easily be constructed to model our language.

The easiest method for constructing a network is to represent the unique components of our rules such as noun, verb,

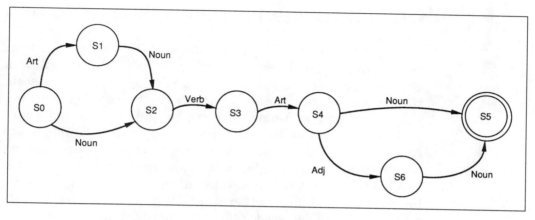

Figure 5.5 A Transition Network

article, etc. as transitions. An example of such a representation is shown in Figure 5.5. Here the initial state is S0. The transitions from states S0 to S2 represent the noun phrase part of the sentence and the transitions from S2 to S5 represent the verb phrase part. This transition network is capable of taking a sentence and determining if that sentence is valid or not according to the grammar rules. If an input sentence starts with an article, then the transition to state S1 is taken, otherwise the sentence must contain a noun as the first word and the transition takes us to S2. There is only one transition from S2 to S3, thus the sentence must have a verb after the noun phrase. The rules for the Noun phrase2 are represented by the remaining transition states S3, S4, S5 or S3, S4, S6, S5. In order for a sentence to be valid, it is necessary to reach the final state S5.

To completely understand how this transition network operates, let us examine what the network does with a simple sentence. Assume you have written this sentence:

```
Mary wants a cat.
```

The network begins at the initial state S0. At this state the word *Mary* is examined and because it is a noun, the noun transition is taken and the new state becomes S2. Here the word *wants*, which is a verb, advances the current state to S3. At this state, the word *a* advances the state to S4 because this word is an article. Finally, the noun *cat* causes the noun transition to be taken and this transition moves us to the final state S5.

As discussed earlier, this technique of breaking a sentence up into words and determining if the individual parts follow a set of predetermined rules is called parsing. The simple state transition network serves as an ideal structure for learning about networks and how they can be applied to parsing languages. Unfortunately, networks such as the simple state transition network easily become cumbersome when working with natural languages because of the complexity of the rules involved. If you want to develop a more sophisticated model for parsing languages, there are other more powerful networks that can be used. One such network is the recursive transition network which is presented next.

The Recursive Transition Network

Recursive transition networks (RTN's) are much better suited for representing natural languages than simple state transition networks. They are actually very similar to state transition networks in the sense that they are composed of states and transitions. RTN's, however, contain transitions which can be networks themselves. This means that RTN's can be defined in a very modular fashion. In the case of natural language processing networks, common transitions such as noun phrases or prepositional phrases can be grouped together to form their own RTN. Because of this type of grouping or organization, it is easier to create networks that model more complex grammar rules.

To gain a better understanding of how RTN's are different from state transition networks, compare the original network from Figure 5.5 to the RTN shown in Figure 5.6. In the original network, you probably noticed that some of the transitions were similar such as the transitions:

    S0 —> S1 —> S2 and S3 —> S4 —> S5

Since these transitions (an article followed by a noun) occur more than once, they can be re-grouped into a new network. The result is the NP network shown in Figure 5.6. This results in simplifying our original network. The only additional requirement in following the state transitions of an RTN is that

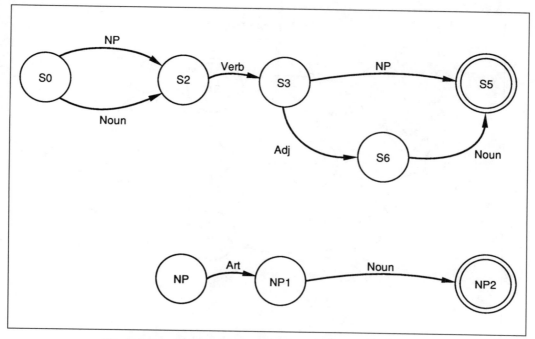

Figure 5.6   Recursive Transition Network

if a transition is itself a network, you must transition through that network until you reach a terminal state. After reaching a terminal state in the sub-network, you can then return to the main network. In this sense RTN's are similar in concept to procedures or subroutines found in a programming language.

Because of their modular nature, RTN's are much easier to construct and program, as you shall see in the following section.

Building an RTN

Programming an RTN is the best way to develop a good understanding of how RTN's work. In this section a workable RTN is presented and you will learn how to create one with Turbo Prolog. The model of the RTN used in this section is shown in Figure 5.7. Note the differences between this network and the state transition network presented earlier. Two of the transitions, NP and PP, are actually networks them-

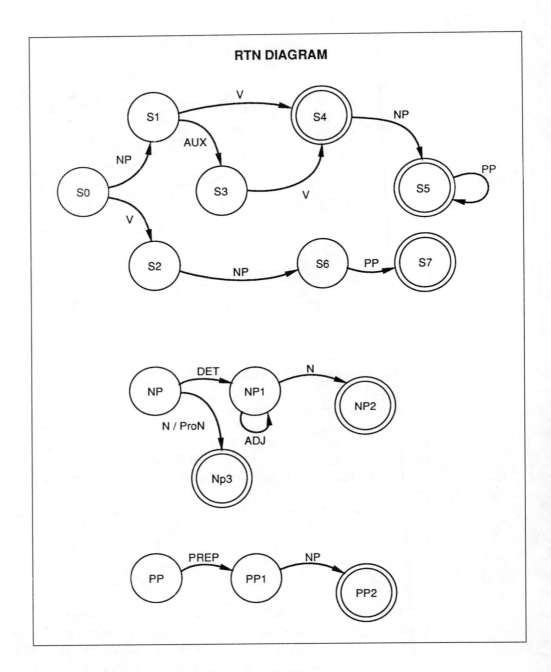

Figure 5.7   RTN for the Sample Grammar

selves. In this network, if you want to move from state S0 to state S1 you must first move through the network labeled NP. The same holds true if you move from S2 to S6 or S4 to S5. The PP network, on the other hand, must be taken before moving from S6 to S7.

The first step in designing a RTN is writing the grammar rules. From the diagram of the RTN, you should be able to come up with the following rules:

```
[1]     Sentence  = NP + VP1
[2]     Sentence  = VP2
[3]     NP        = Noun | Pronoun
[4]     NP        = Determiner + Adjective + Noun
[5]     NP        = Determiner + Noun
[6]     VP2       = Verb + NP + PP
[7]     VP1       = Auxiliary Verb + Verb + NP + (PP)
[8]     VP1       = Verb + NP + (PP)
[9]     PP        = Prep + NP
```

These rules are not very complex; however, you should review them before continuing on. The VP1 in rule 1 stands for Verb Phrase1 which is represented by the states S1, S3, S4, and S5 in the RTN diagram. VP2 is Verb Phrase2 and it is represented by states S2, S6, and S7. In rules 7 and 8, the prepositional phrase, PP, is enclosed in the "( )" to indicate that it is an optional part. The tree representation of these rules is shown in Figure 5.8.

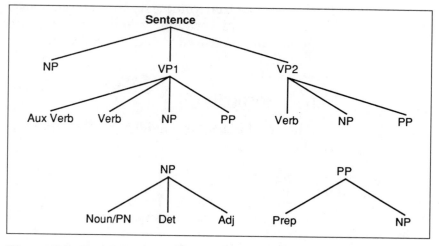

Figure 5.8 Tree Representation of the Sample Grammar Rules

Now that the grammar is defined, the next step is to determine the vocabulary. There are seven distinct types of words in our grammar: determiners, pronouns, nouns, auxiliary verbs, verbs, prepositions, and adjectives. Let us choose some words for these different classifications:

Determiners	Pronouns	Nouns	Aux Verbs	Verbs	Prep	Adj
a	I	files	can	is	on	hard
the	you	disk	will	are	at	big
that		boy		reads	in	happy
		newspaper		program		
		computer		run		
		book		execute		
		magazine				
		table				

Keep in mind that this is not a very large vocabulary and therefore the sentences you will be able to process with the RTN will be limited. Nevertheless, there are enough words to help you understand the important concepts in processing English sentences with the RTN. Of course, you can easily add new words to the RTN program to increase its vocabulary. Using the grammar rules and the defined vocabulary you can create sentences such as:

```
The boy can program the big computer.
Are the files on the hard disk.
```

Each sentence that you create must be composed of the words from the special vocabulary and must end with a period. If these conditions are not met, the RTN will not recognize the sentence.

Implementing the RTN

The vocabulary for our RTN can be stored as a set of facts as shown:

```
word_type("a", det).
word_type("the", det).
word_type("that", det).
word_type("I", pronoun).
word_type("you", pronoun).
word_type("files", noun).
```

```
word_type("disk", noun).
word_type("boy", noun).
word_type("newspaper", noun).
word_type("computer", noun).
word_type("book", noun).
word_type("magazine", noun).
word_type("table", noun).
word_type("can", aux).
word_type("will", aux).
word_type("is", verb).
word_type("are", verb).
word_type("reads", verb).
word_type("programs", verb).
word_type("run", verb).
word_type("execute", verb).
word_type("on", prep).
word_type("at", prep).
word_type("in", prep).
word_type("hard", adj).
word_type("big", adj).
word_type("happy", adj).
```

The actual word is represented as a string and its corresponding type is represented as a symbol. The type definition for
"word_type" is:

```
predicates
  word_type(string, symbol)
```

If you want to add new words you can do so at any time as long
as the word is one of the defined types. Thus, if you want to
add the word *typewriter*, which is a noun, to your database,
include the clause:

```
word_type("typewriter", noun).
```

The top level clause for the RTN is called run and is shown
here:

```
run:-
set_state(s0),
write("The RTN will analyze your sentence"), nl,
write("Please type in your sentence >>"),
readln(Sent),
analyze(Sent),
```

```
            write("Your sentence is ok"),nl,
            clear_state.

        run:-
            write("Your sentence has failed"),nl,
            clear_state.
```

Run initializes the current state to s0 which is the initial state for the RTN. This clause is also responsible for reading in the input sentence and calling the analyze clause which is the process responsible for handling the parsing operation of the sentence. If the analyze clause succeeds, then the message:

```
Your sentence is ok
```

is displayed. Otherwise the main clause run will fail and you will see the message:

```
Your sentence has failed
```

The last clause called, clear_state, is responsible for retracting the previous assertions made to the current_state database. This action is necessary in order for the RTN to operate correctly if you run it a second time.

A database clause is used to store the present transition state as the RTN is traveled. Its definition is:

```
database
    current_state(states)
```

The program updates the state variable as it moves around the RTN by calling the clause set_state coded as:

```
set_state(Sn):-
    asserta(current_state(Sn)).
```

When this clause is called, the current state is stored away in the database through the asserta clause. States are retrieved from the state database by calling get_state which is coded as:

```
get_state(Sn):-
    current_state(Sn).
```

This clause simply reads the current contents of the state database.

As mentioned earlier, the clause responsible for processing the sentence is analyze. This clause consists of two parts:

```
analyze(S):-
    S = ".",
    final_state(_).
```

```
analyze(S):-
  get_state(New_state), !,
  transition(New_state, S, S1),
  analyze(S1).
```

The first clause tests to see if the end of the sentence has been reached by checking to see if the input string is equal to the "." (the end of sentence marker). If that is so, then the clause final_state is called which determines if the RTN is in one of its final states. If the RTN is not in a final state, then the sentence fails, otherwise the sentence is accepted—remember that the RTN must be in one of its final states in order for it to accept an input string.

The second part of analyze is responsible for directing the transition states of the RTN by calling the clause transition. Analyze is recursive and every time it calls transition with the variables:

```
transition(New_state, S, S1)
```

it passes the current state New_state, and the current sentence S. The part of the sentence which is left after the next transition state is taken is returned in S1. This new sentence is then passed to analyze recursively.

As an example, assume that our sentence is:

```
are the files on the hard disk.
```

and thus the first call to the analyze clause would be:

```
analyze("are the files on the hard disk")
```

When anaylze makes its first call to transition the parameters would be:

```
transition(s0, "are the files on the hard disk", S1)
```

This indicates that the RTN is in the initial state, S0. After the transition clause is completed, the variable S1 would contain the value:

```
"the files on the hard disk"
```

This new value would then be passed to analyze for further processing. Of course, the current state of the transition network would be changed in the process.

The transition clauses are divided up into three groups of clauses, each representing part of the RTN diagram from Figure 5.7. The three groups consist of main transitions, noun phrase transitions, and prepositional phrase transitions. The main transitions are coded as:

```
transition(sO, Sa, Sb):-
    get_token(Sa, W, Sb),
    word_type(W, verb),
    set_state(s2).

transition(sO, Sa, Sb):-
    check_NP(np, Sa, Sb),
    set_state(s1).

transition(s1, Sa, Sb):-
    get_token(Sa, W, Sb),
    word_type(W, aux),
    set_state(s3).

transition(s1, Sa, Sb):-
    get_token(Sa, W, Sb),
    word_type(W, verb),
    set_state(s4).

transition(s2, Sa, Sb):-
    check_NP(np, Sa, Sb),
    set_state(s6).

transition(s3, Sa, Sb):-
    get_token(Sa, W, Sb),
    word_type(W, verb),
    set_state(s4).

transition(s4, Sa, Sb):-
    check_NP(np, Sa, Sb),
    set_state(s5).

transition(s5, Sa, Sb):-
    check_PP(pp, Sa, Sb).

transition(s6, Sa, Sb):-
    check_PP(pp, Sa, Sb),
    set_state(s7).
```

These clauses direct the movement from one transition state to another state within the main RTN. There are two types of transitions available. One controls the movement within the main network and the other is responsible for accessing the other networks. The first is represented by a transition such as:

```
transition(s0, Sa, Sb):-
    get_token(Sa, W, Sb),
    word_type(W, verb),
    set_state(s2).
```

Here the basic operations of this type of transition are:

```
i)    get the first word from the current sentence phrase
ii)   test the word to see if it is of the correct type
iii)  move to the next transition state if the word
      matches the transition
```

The get_token clause is responsible for extracting the first word or token from a string of words. The clause is written using a few of the string processing tools developed in Chapter 3:

```
get_token(S1, W, S2):-
    get_position(S1, Pos), !,
    L = Pos - 1,
    strleftx(S1, W, L ),
    R = Pos + 1,
    strrightx(S1, S2, R).
```

The clause get_position searches for either a space or a period and returns its position in the string. This clause uses one of the standard tools strcfind which was constructed in Chapter 3. Strcfind scans a string for a specified character and returns the index position of the match. The get_position clause is:

```
get_position(S1, Pos):-       /* search for blank */
    strcfind(S1, ` `, Pos).

get_position(S1, Pos):-       /* search for period */
    strcfind(S1, `.`, Pos).
```

Once get_token determines the location of the space or period delimiter, it makes calls to two of the string tools from Chapter 3: strleftx which extracts the left-most part of a string, and strrightx which extracts the right-most part. To get a better idea of how get_token works, let us look at an example.

Assume that the string sent to get_token is:

```
"the dogs are playing in the yard tonight"
```

The clause get_position would return back an index of 4 for the space between "the" and "dogs." This index value is decreased by 1 with the statement:

```
L = Pos - 1
```

and the call:

```
strleftx("the dogs are ...", W, 3)
```

would bind the variable W to the word "the." It is also necessary to skip over the first word and return the rest of the phrase and the clause:

```
strrightx("the dogs are ..., S2, R)
```

will bind the variable to the rest of the string, "dogs are... tonight." Note the value of R would be 5 in this example because of the statement:

```
R = Pos + 1
```

As mentioned earlier, there are two types of transition clauses and the second type is represented by the following:

```
transition(s0, Sa, Sb):-
   check_NP(np, Sa, Sb),
   set_state(s1).
```

This transition jumps from the main RTN to the noun phrase RTN. Because of this modular nature, it would not be very difficult to add other networks and thus increase the complexity of the types of sentences the RTN can process. This, of course, is one of the major advantages of using the RTN. The check_NP clause is called from this transition clause and if it is successful then the current state is changed. Check_NP represents a separate RTN with its own initial and terminal states as you can see from the following code:

```
check_NP(np2, Sc, Sb):- Sb = Sc, !.

check_NP(np3, Sc, Sb):- Sb = Sc, !.

check_NP(St, Sa, Sb):-
   transition(St, Sa, Sc),
```

```
        get_state(Ns),
        check_NP(Ns, Sc, Sb), !.
```

The first two clauses actually test to see if a terminal state for this RTN has been reached. If not, the third clause is taken and calls itself recursively until either a terminal state is found or a word in the input string fails to match with a transition state. The PP network must also be a separate RTN and its code is similar to that of the NP RTN:

```
check_PP(pp2, Sc, Sb):- Sb = Sc, !.
check_PP(St, Sa, Sb):-
        transition(St, Sa, Sc),
        get_state(Ns),
        check_NP(Ns, Sc, Sb), !.
```

Finally, here is the complete code for the NP RTN transitions:

```
transition(np, Sa, Sb):-
        get_token(Sa, W, Sb),
        word_type(W, det),
        set_state(np1).

transition(np, Sa, Sb):-
        get_token(Sa, W, Sb),
        word_type(W, noun),
        set_state(np3)

transition(np, Sa, Sb):-
        get_token(Sa, W, Sb),
        word_type(W, pronoun),
        set_state(np3).

transition(np1, Sa, Sb):-
        get_token(Sa, W, Sb),
        word_type(W, noun),
        set_state(np2)
transition(np1, Sa, Sb):-
        get_token(Sa, W, Sb),
        word_type(W, adj).
```

And the code for the PP RTN transitions:

```
transition(pp, Sa, Sb):-
        get_token(Sa, W, Sb),
```

```
        word_type(W, prep),
        set_state(pp1).
    transition(pp1, Sa, Sb):-
        check_NP(np, Sa, Sb),
        set_state(pp2).
```

The complete code for the RTN English sentence parser is included next (Listing 5.1). The program uses three string processing tools from Chapter 3: strleftx, strrightx, and strcfind. These tools are included in the program with the code:

```
include "strcfind.pro"
include "strleftx.pro"
include "strrightx.pro"
```

To get a better idea of how this program works, you should type it in and compile it with the Turbo Prolog system. When you execute the program and the goal window appears, enter the main clause:

```
run.
```

to start the RTN. The program will ask you to type in your sentence and then will proceed to analyze it. If the sentence is valid, the message:

```
Your sentence is ok
```

will be displayed, otherwise you will see the message:

```
Your sentence has failed.
```

Listing 5.1

```
        /* RTN Program Code 5-1 */
domains

    states = symbol        /* transition states */
    class = symbol         /* word classification */

database

    current_state(states)    /* transition state variable */

/*********** String processing tools *************/
include "strcfind.pro"    /* search for a character */
include "strleftx.pro"    /* extract left most characters */
include "strrightx.pro"   /* extract right most characters */
```

predicates

```
run                                    /* top level predicate      */
clear_state                            /* resets the state database */
set_state(states)                      /* saves state in database   */
get_state(states)                      /* gets state from database  */
final_state(states)                    /* the terminal states       */
get_position(string, integer)          /* finds word position        */
get_token(string, string, string)      /* gets the current word     */
analyze(string)                        /* parses the sentence       */
transition(states, string, string)     /* transition rule           */
check_NP(states, string, string)       /* noun phrase network       */
check_PP(states, string, string)       /* prep. phrase network      */
word_type(string,class)                /* word dictionary           */
```

clauses

```
run:-
set_state(s0),                                 /* initialize state */
write("The RTN will analyze your sentence"), nl,
write("Please type in your sentence >>"),
readln(Sent),
analyze(Sent),
write("Your sentence is ok"),nl,
clear_state.


run:-
write("Your sentence has failed"),nl,
clear_state.

final_state(s4):-
    current_state(s4).

final_state(s5):-
    current_state(s5).

final_state(s7):-
    current_state(s7).

set_state(Sn):-                 /* save current transition state */
    asserta(current_state(Sn)).

 get_state(Sn):-                /* get current transition state */
    current_state(Sn).

clear_state:-
    retract(current_state(_)),    /* restore state database */
    fail.
```

(continued)

```
    clear_state.

    get_position(S1, Pos):-            /* search for blank */
        strcfind(S1, ' ', Pos).

    get_position(S1, Pos):-            /* search for period */
        strcfind(S1, '.', Pos).

    get_token(S1, W, S2):-             /* get token word from sentence */
        get_position(S1, Pos), !,
        L = Pos - 1,
        strleftx(S1, W, L ),
        R = Pos + 1,
        strrightx(S1, S2, R).

/***********   The sentence analyzer  ************/

    analyze(S):-                       /* analyzes the sentence by following the */
                                       /* transition network       */
        S = ".",
        final_state(_).

    analyze(S):-
        get_state(New_state), !,       /* determine present state */
        transition(New_state, S, S1),
        analyze(S1).


/*****************************************************************/
/*      Main Transitions      */

    transition(s0, Sa, Sb):-
        get_token(Sa, W, Sb),
        word_type(W, verb),
        set_state(s2).

    transition(s0, Sa, Sb):-
        check_NP(np, Sa, Sb),
        set_state(s1).

    transition(s1, Sa, Sb):-
        get_token(Sa, W, Sb),
        word_type(W, aux),
        set_state(s3).

    transition(s1, Sa, Sb):-
        get_token(Sa, W, Sb),
        word_type(W, verb),
        set_state(s4).

    transition(s2, Sa, Sb):-
        check_NP(np, Sa, Sb),
        set_state(s6).
```

```
        transition(s3, Sa, Sb):-
            get_token(Sa, W, Sb),
            word_type(W, verb),
            set_state(s4).

        transition(s4, Sa, Sb):-
            check_NP(np, Sa, Sb),
            set_state(s5).

        transition(s5, Sa, Sb):-
            check_PP(pp, Sa, Sb).

        transition(s6, Sa, Sb):-
            check_PP(pp, Sa, Sb),
            set_state(s7).

/*******************************************************************/
/* Noun phrase transitions    */

        transition(np, Sa, Sb):-
            get_token(Sa, W, Sb),
            word_type(W, det),
            set_state(np1).

        transition(np, Sa, Sb):-
            get_token(Sa, W, Sb),
            word_type(W, noun),
            set_state(np3).

        transition(np, Sa, Sb):-
            get_token(Sa, W, Sb),
            word_type(W, pronoun),
            set_state(np3).

        transition(np1, Sa, Sb):-
            get_token(Sa, W, Sb),
            word_type(W, noun),
            set_state(np2).

        transition(np1, Sa, Sb):-
            get_token(Sa, W, Sb),
            word_type(W, adj).

/*******************************************************************/
/*   Prepositional phrase transitions      */

        transition(pp, Sa, Sb):-
            get_token(Sa, W, Sb),
            word_type(W, prep),
            set_state(pp1).

        transition(pp1, Sa, Sb):-
            check_NP(np, Sa, Sb),
            set_state(pp2).
```

(continued)

```
/***************************************************************/
/*   NP RTN    */

    check_NP(np2, Sc, Sb):- Sb = Sc, !.

    check_NP(np3, Sc, Sb):- Sb = Sc, !.

    check_NP(St, Sa, Sb):-
        transition(St, Sa, Sc),
        get_state(Ns),
        check_NP(Ns, Sc, Sb), !.

/****************************************************************/
/*  PP RTN      */

    check_PP(pp2, Sc, Sb):- Sb = Sc, !.

    check_PP(St, Sa, Sb):-
        transition(St, Sa, Sc),
        get_state(Ns),
        check_NP(Ns, Sc, Sb), !.


/*+++++++++++++++++++++++++++++++++++++++++++++++++++++++++++++++ */
/*   words....    */

        word_type("a", det).
        word_type("the", det).
        word_type("that", det).
        word_type("I", pronoun).
        word_type("you", pronoun).
        word_type("files", noun).
        word_type("disk", noun).
        word_type("boy", noun).
        word_type("newspaper", noun).
        word_type("computer", noun).
        word_type("book", noun).
        word_type("magazine", noun).
        word_type("table", noun).
        word_type("can", aux).
        word_type("will", aux).
        word_type("is", verb).
        word_type("are", verb).
        word_type("reads", verb).
        word_type("programs", verb).
        word_type("run", verb).
        word_type("execute", verb).
        word_type("on", prep).
        word_type("at", prep).
        word_type("in", prep).
        word_type("hard", adj).
        word_type("big", adj).
        word_type("happy", adj).
```

Summary of the RTN

The advantages of the RTN over the simple state transition network should be easily seen. Because of the complexity of the English language, it is important to have a model for language processing which can be easily expandable. Grammar rules can be added to the RTN easily as has been shown, and new words can be added to increase the vocabulary of the RTN. Because of its flexibility, the RTN provides a good model for parsing sentences.

The main drawback of the RTN for natural language processing is that it is not really capable of understanding anything about the sentences that it analyzes. Of course, this is not a simple task, but it might be more helpful to develop a language processor that can tell us something about the structure and organization of the sentences it analyzes.

The Augmented Transition Network

The problem with the RTN is that it only accepts or rejects sentences and it does not tell us anything about the structure or meaning of the sentences. A useful natural language processing program should be able to perform a complete analysis on a sentence and to use the results to carry out some operation.

In this section, the augmented transition network (ATN), which is another type of network developed for analyzing natural languages, will be presented. The ATN is actually a natural extension of the RTN presented earlier. ATN's are important because not only are they able to decide if an English sentence is grammatical or not, they are also able to classify the sentence structures and recreate a sentence. For example, if you provided the following sentence to an ATN:

```
John builds houses in California.
```

the ATN could tell you that the sentence is structured as:

```
[ [NP John] [VP builds [NP houses] [PP in [NP California] ] ] ]
```

This notation tells you that the sentence consists of the noun phrase *John* and the verb phrase *builds houses in California*. The verb phrase itself can be broken up into the verb *builds*, the noun phrase *houses*, and the prepositional phrase *in Cali-*

fornia. The information provided here is essentially the same information that could be represented by the type of parse tree shown earlier in Figure 5.2. Of course, once this information is obtained it could be used by a natural language processing program to perform further analysis.

Building the ATN

The ATN is structurally very similar to the RTN. It utilizes the concepts of states and transitions and can also be designed in a modular fashion. Therefore, an ATN can be composed of other ATN's. However, these new networks must contain place holders to store the structural parts of a sentence while being analyzed.

The RTN program developed earlier can be used as the starting point for the new ATN program. To simplify the coding of the ATN, the same grammar from our RTN model presented in Figure 5.7 will be used. However, before you begin coding the ATN, it is important to learn about the fundamental principles behind the ATN. The ATN introduces some new concepts and terminology which are presented next.

In order to store the structural parts of a sentence as it is parsed, the ATN uses registers. A register is actually a memory location which acts as a place holder. Each register is responsible for holding a structural element or phrase such as a noun, verb, adjective, noun phrase, verb phrase, etc. After a sentence is analyzed by the ATN, these registers are used to construct the sentence. The registers used in the ATN program are shown in Figure 5.9.

The registers play a major part in the operation of the ATN. The ATN uses a different specification grammar than the RTN. The registers add a new level of complexity; however, most of the register operations consist simply of reading and writing values. In order to fully understand how these registers are used, it would be helpful for us to create a set of grammar rules for our ATN program.

Writing ATN Grammar Rules

The rules necessary for the ATN are more complex than the rules used in our RTN program, even though both of the

Registers for ATN

ADJ	Adjective Register
AUX	Auxiliary Verb Register
DET	Determiner Register
NOUN	Noun Register
NP	Noun Phrase Register
OBJ	Object Register
PP	Prepositional Phrase Register
PREP	Preposition Register
SUBJ	Subject Register
TYPE	Sentence Type Register
VERB	Verb Register
VP	Verb Phrase Register

Figure 5.9   Registers Used in the ATN Program

networks accept the same sentences. The complete set of rules are shown here:

```
                Rules for ATN Grammar
      Start:
           Call NP
           (True)
                 Set Register    TYPE = DECL
                 Set Register    SUBJ = Str
                 Call S1
                 Build    Result = [TYPE SUBJ VP]

           (False)
                 Set Register    TYPE = QUEST
                 Set Register    VERB = Input_Word
                 Call S2
                 Build    Result = [TYPE VP]

      S1:
           Call VP
                 Set Register    VP = Str
                 Return
```

```
S2:
     Call NP
          Set Register        OBJ = Str
          Goto S6
          Build      Str =    ["VP" VERB OBJ PP]
          Set Register        VP = Str
          Return

NP:
     IF Input_Word = Det
          Set Register               DET = Input_Word
          Set Register               ADJ = Null
          Goto NP1

     ELSE IF Input_Word = Noun/Pronoun
          Set Register               NOUN = Input_Word
          Set Register               ADJ  = Null
          Goto NP2

NP1:
     IF Input_Word = Adj
          Append Register            ADJ = ADJ + Input_Word
          Goto NP1

     ELSE IF Input_Word = Noun
          Set Register               NOUN = Input_Word
          Goto NP2

NP2:
     Build      Str = ["NP" DET ADJ NOUN]
     Return

VP:
     IF Input_Word = Verb
          Set Register               VERB = Input_Word
          Set Register               AUX  = Null
          Goto S4

     ELSE IF Input_Word = Aux
          Set Register               AUX = Input_Word


          Goto S3:
```

```
S3
      IF Input_Word = Verb
            Set Register             VERB = Input_Word
            Goto S4

S4:
      IF Input_Word = Null
            Build Str = ["VP" AUX VERB]
            Return

      ELSE
            Test NP
              Set Register           OBJ = Str
              Set Register           PP  = Null
            Goto S5

S5:
      IF Input_Word = Null
            Build  Str = ["VP" AUX VERB OBJ PP]
            Return

      ELSE
            Test PP
              Append Register        PP = PP + Str
            Goto S5

S6:
      Test PP
            Set Register             PP = Str
            Return

PP:

      IF Input_word = Prep
            Set Register             PREP = Input_Word
            Goto PP1

PP1:
      Call NP
            Set Register             NP = Str
            Goto PP2

PP2:
      Build     Str = ["PP" PREP NP]
```

Included in the rules is the information about how the different registers are used. There are three main operations relating to the registers that are necessary to understand. In our rules, a statement such as:

```
Set Register TYPE = DECL
```

performs the task of assigning a value to a register. In this case, the TYPE register is assigned the value "DECL" indicating that the sentence is a declarative sentence and not a question. The other main operation used to update the contents of a register is the Append operator. As an example, consider this statement:

```
Append Register ADJ = ADJ + Input_word
```

which updates the ADJ register by appending its previous contents with a new value. This operation is needed because, according to our grammar rules, it is possible to generate sentences which contain multiple adjectives such as:

```
The big happy boy programs the computer.
```

Finally, the operation responsible for building phrases from the contents of the registers is the Build operation. For example, the statement:

```
Build Result = [TYPE SUBJ VP]
```

creates a phrase out of the registers TYPE, SUBJ, VP.

Perhaps the best way to understand how these rules work is to look at an example. Assume that you have the following sentence:

```
The crazy computer programs the man.
```

To begin, look at the first set of rules:

```
Start:
        Call NP
        (True)
                Set Register    TYPE = DECL
                Set Register    SUBJ = Str
                Call S1
                Build       Result = [TYPE SUBJ VP]

        (False)
                Set Register    TYPE = QUEST
                Set Register    VERB = Input_Word
```

```
                    Call S2
                    Build       Result = [TYPE VP]
```

The label "Start:" marks the beginning of the first group of
rules. The first operation, represented by the statement "Call
NP" consists of testing the NP (noun phrase) network. If the
first phrase of our sentence is a noun phrase then the NP network will be accessed. After the call to the NP network, the
sentence TYPE register is set to "DECL" and the Subject register, SUBJ, is set to the noun phrase built in the NP network.
If the NP network is called with our example sentence, the following operations will take place: The first input word is "The"
which is a determiner and therefore the following register as-
signments are made:

```
     Set Register       DET = Input_Word
     Set Register       ADJ = Null
```

The following step is to move to the next transition, NP1, and
update the ADJ register with the input word "crazy." As
shown in the grammar rules, the operation is:

```
     Append Register ADJ = ADJ + Input_Word
```

Finally, the last word of the noun phrase, "computer," is
stored in the NOUN register. At this point, there are no more
words left in the noun phrase. Therefore, the final rule of the
NP network:

```
     NP2:
            Build       Str = ["NP" DET ADJ NOUN]
            Return
```

is encountered. The phrase consisting of the three registers,
DET, ADJ, and NOUN are built. This new phrase consists of:

```
     Str = [NP The crazy computer]
```

This completes the processing of our NP network. The return
statement takes us back to the first rule where the SUBJ register is set to the value of the variable Str.

The next step is to process the verb phrase. The statement,
Call S1, is responsible for taking us to the next node of the
network represented as:

```
     S1:
       Call VP
            Set Register     VP = Str
            Return
```

The processing of the verb phrase is very similar to the steps involved in building the noun phrase for our sample sentence. At this point you might want to trace through the operation of the VP network to fully understand how the registers are used and how the verb phrase is constructed. Keep in mind that the processing of these rules is simply a matter of traveling through the network and manipulating the registers. The result after processing the verb phrase stored in the VP register turns out to be:

```
[VP programs [NP the man]]
```

The final Build operation is responsible for constructing the sentence. This operation:

```
Build    Result = [TYPE SUBJ VP]
```

produces:

```
[DECL [NP The crazy computer] [VP programs [NP the man]]]
```

As you can see, the processing of these rules is not much different than following the RTN presented in the previous section. The major difference consists of the technique of storing and building phrases as the sentence is analyzed. Once you familiarize yourself with the simple register operations, the actual implementation of the ATN should not be difficult. In the following section, all of the concepts developed here will be put together so that a working ATN can be written in Turbo Prolog.

Implementing the ATN

The first step in coding the ATN program is to determine how the registers should be implemented. To keep the design of the program simple, database clauses will be used to store and read the registers. Here is the code for this representation:

```
database
        type_reg(string)         /* sentence type register   */
        np_reg(string)           /* noun phrase register      */
        verb_reg(string)         /* verb register             */
        subj_reg(string)         /* subject register          */
        obj_reg(string)          /* object register           */
```

```
aux_reg(string)          /* auxiliary verb register */
pp_reg(string)           /* prep phrase register    */
prep_reg(string)         /* preposition register    */
vp_reg(string)           /* verb phrase register    */
det_reg(string)          /* determiner register     */
adj_reg(string)          /* adjective register      */
noun_reg(string)         /* noun register           */
```

Note that all of the sentence elements from our grammar such as verb, noun, noun phrase, preposition, etc. are represented. The instructions for updating registers are contained within the transition clauses which are slightly modified from the RTN program. For example, one of the transitions for the start state S0 is now written as:

```
transition(s0, Sa, Sb):-
 check_NP(np, Sa, Sb),
 asserta(type_reg("DECL")),     /* store sentence type*/
 build_phrase(np, Str),
 asserta(subj_reg(Str)),        /* store subject */
 set_state(s1).
```

The clause asserta(type_reg("DECL")) updates the type register and the clause asserta(subj_reg(Str)) updates the subject register. In the ATN program, each transition clause now contains one or more of these assertions to the register database. With this implementation, accessing the registers is simply a matter of reading the database clauses or asserting clauses.

The other major addition to the ATN program are the build_phrase clauses shown here:

```
    build_phrase(np, Str):-
      det_reg(Detr),
      adj_reg(Adjr),
      noun_reg(Nounr),
      get_template(np,T),
      fill_template(T, Detr, T1),
      fill_template(T1, Adjr, T2),
      fill_template(T2, Nounr, Str).

    build_phrase(vp1, Str):-
      aux_reg(Auxr),
      verb_reg(Verbr),
      get_template(vp, T),
      fill_template(T, Auxr, T1),
      fill_template(T1, Verbr, Str).
```

```
build_phrase(vp2, Str):-
  aux_reg(Auxr),
  verb_reg(Verbr),
  obj_reg(Objr),
  pp_reg(Ppr),
  get_template(vp, T),
  fill_template(T, Auxr, T1),
  fill_template(T1, Verbr, T2),
  fill_template(T2, Objr, T3),
  fill_template(T3, Ppr, Str).

build_phrase(pp, Str):-
  prep_reg(Prepr),
  np_reg(Npr),
  get_template(pp, T),
  fill_template(T, Prepr, T1),
  fill_template(T1, Npr, Str)

build_phrase(s, Str):-
  type_reg(Typr),
  subj_reg(Subjr),
  vp_reg(Vpr),
  get_template(s, T),
  fill_template(T, Typr, T1),
  fill_template(T1, Subjr, T2),
  fill_template(T2, Vpr, Str).

build_phrase(s1, Str):-
  type_reg(Typr),
  vp_reg(Vpr),
  get_template(s, T),
  fill_template(T, Typr, T1),
  fill_template(T1, Vpr, Str).
```

These clauses are used for constructing phrases from the registers. Each clause contains the rules for creating a specified phrase such as a noun phrase, verb phrase, or an entire sentence phrase. In each clause definition, the first argument indicates the phrase type to be built and the second argument is used to store the result. Build_phrase is normally called from one of the transition clauses which represent states that are phrase terminators. These states are s1, s4, s5, s6, and s7. As an example, assume the ATN is processing the sentence:

```
The boy programs.
```

After the ATN processes the word "boy," the current transition state would be s1. At this point, build_phrase would be called and the noun phrase, "The boy" would be built from the two registers det_reg and noun_reg. The result would be placed in the np_reg as:

```
[NP The boy]
```

Build_phrase is also called from the clause check_build. Check_build is responsible for testing to see if the sentence terminator "." is encountered at one of the final states. Therefore, whenever one of the states s4 or s5 is reached, check_build is called. As shown here, this clause will construct the appropriate sentence phrase and store it in the database:

```
check_build(Type, S):-
   S = ".",
   build_phrase(Type, Str),
   asserta(vp_reg(Str)).

check_build(_,_).
```

To construct sentence phrases, build_phrase actually uses two local clauses, get_template and fill_template. Get_template contains the phrase templates:

```
get_template(np, "[NP]").
get_template(vp, "[VP]").
get_template(pp, "[PP]").
get_template(s, "[]").
```

and fill_template is responsible for filling these templates with phrases. The code for these clauses is:

```
fill_template(T, Str, Result):-
   Str= "",
   Result = T.

fill_template(T, Str, Result):-
   strclfind(T, ']', P),
   strsi(T, " ", P, T1),
   Pos = P + 1,
   strsi(T1, Str, Pos, Result).
```

Note that strclfind and strsi, two of the string processing tools from Chapter 3, are used here. Remember that strclfind returns the position of the last occurrence of a specified character in a string. Therefore, in this application, strclfind will look for the very last right bracket. The other clause, strsi, is used to insert a phrase inside a template.

The only other modification that has been made to our original program is the exchange of the clear_state clause with the clear_dbase clause. Our new program makes many new assertions to the database and it is necessary to retract these assertions before the program terminates. This action is done at the end of the main clause run. If the database clauses are not retracted, the ATN program will not function correctly if it is run from the goal window without compilation. Clear_dbase is a simple clause consisting only of retractions as shown:

```
clear_dbase:-
   retract(_),
   fail.

clear_dbase.
```

The first clause retracts all of the stored variables in the database. The statement "retract(_)" performs this operation.

At this point you should enter in the ATN program and test it out on some sentences. The complete code is included next. After you type in the program, compile it and select the RUN option from the Turbo Prolog working menu. The goal window should appear and you can start the ATN by typing in the main clause:

```
run.
```

Here is the complete program:

Listing 5.2

```
                    /* ATN Program  Code 5-2   */
domains

   states = symbol      /* transition states */
   class = symbol       /* word classification */

database

   current_state(states)    /* transition state variable */
```

```
        type_reg(string)         /* sentence type register */
        np_reg(string)           /* noun phrase register   */
        verb_reg(string)         /* verb register          */
        subj_reg(string)         /* subject register       */
        obj_reg(string)          /* object register        */
        aux_reg(string)          /* auxilary verb register */
        pp_reg(string)           /* prep phrase register    */
        prep_reg(string)         /* preposition register   */
        vp_reg(string)           /* verb phrase register    */
        det_reg(string)          /* determiner register    */
        adj_reg(string)          /* adjective register     */
        noun_reg(string)         /* noun register          */


/*********** String processing tools *************/

include "strleftx.pro"      /* extract left most characters */
include "strrightx.pro"     /* extract right most characters */
include "strsi.pro"
include "strclfin.pro"

predicates

    run                                /* top level predicate    */
    clear_dbase                        /* resets the full database */
    set_state(states)                  /* saves state in database */
    get_state(states)                  /* gets state from database */
    final_state(states)                /* the terminal states    */
    get_position(string, integer)      /* finds word position     */
    get_token(string, string, string)  /* gets the current word   */
    analyze(string)                    /* parses the sentence     */
    transition(states, string, string) /* transition rule         */
    check_NP(states, string, string)   /* noun phrase network     */
    check_PP(states, string, string)   /* prep. phrase network    */
    word_type(string,class)            /* word dictionary         */

    get_template(symbol, string)
    fill_template(string, string, string)
    build_phrase(symbol, string)
    check_build(symbol, string)

clauses

    run:-
    set_state(s0),                                  /* initialize state */
    write("The ATN will analyze your sentence"), nl,
    write("Please type in your sentence >>"),
    readln(Sent),
    analyze(Sent),
    write("Your sentence is ok"),nl,
    clear_dbase.
```

(continued)

```
run:-
write("Your sentence has failed"),nl,
clear_dbase.

final_state(s4):-
    current_state(s4),
    build_phrase(s, Str),
    write(Str), nl.

final_state(s5):-
    current_state(s5),
    build_phrase(s, Str),
    write(Str), nl.

final_state(s7):-
    current_state(s7),
    build_phrase(s1, Str),
    write(Str), nl.

set_state(Sn):-                       /* save current transition state */
    asserta(current_state(Sn)).

get_state(Sn):-                       /* get current transition state */
    current_state(Sn).

clear_dbase:-
    retract(_),                       /* restore database */
    fail.

clear_dbase.

get_position(S1, Pos):-               /* search for blank */
    strcfind(S1, ' ', Pos).

get_position(S1, Pos):-               /* search for period */
    strcfind(S1, '.', Pos).

get_token(S1, W, S2):-                /* get token word from sentence */
    get_position(S1, Pos), !,
    L = Pos - 1,
    strleftx(S1, W, L ),
    R = Pos + 1,
    strrightx(S1, S2, R).

/*********** The sentence analyzer ***********/
analyze(S):-                /* analyzes the sentence by following the */
                            /* transition network      */

    S = ".",
    final_state(_).

analyze(S):-
    get_state(New_state), !,           /* determine present state */
    transition(New_state, S, S1), !,
    analyze(S1).
```

```
/*************************************************************************/
/*      Main Transitions      */

  transition(s0, Sa, Sb):-
     get_token(Sa, W, Sb),
     word_type(W, verb),
     asserta(type_reg("QUEST")),        /* store snentence type */
     asserta(verb_reg(W)),              /* store verb        */
     asserta(aux_reg("")),
     set_state(s2).

  transition(s0, Sa, Sb):-
     check_NP(np, Sa, Sb),
     asserta(type_reg("DECL")),          /* store sentence type */
     build_phrase(np, Str),
     asserta(subj_reg(Str)),              /* store subject      */
     set_state(s1).

  transition(s1, Sa, Sb):-
     get_token(Sa, W, Sb),
     word_type(W, aux),
     asserta(aux_reg(W)),                 /* store auxilary verb */
     set_state(s3).

  transition(s1, Sa, Sb):-
     get_token(Sa, W, Sb),
     word_type(W, verb),
     asserta(aux_reg("")),
     asserta(verb_reg(W)),                /* store verb    */
     set_state(s4),
     check_build(vp1, Sb).

  transition(s2, Sa, Sb):-
     check_NP(np, Sa, Sb),
     build_phrase(np, Str),
     asserta(obj_reg(Str)),               /* store object */
     set_state(s6).

  transition(s3, Sa, Sb):-
     get_token(Sa, W, Sb),
     word_type(W, verb),
     asserta(verb_reg(W)),                /* store verb  */
     set_state(s4),
     check_build(vp2, Sb).

  transition(s4, Sa, Sb):-
     check_NP(np, Sa, Sb),
     build_phrase(np, Str),
     asserta(obj_reg(Str)),               /* store object   */
     asserta(pp_reg("")),
     set_state(s5),
     check_build(vp2, Sb).
```

(continued)

```
    transition(s5, Sa, Sb):-
        check_PP(pp, Sa, Sb),
        build_phrase(pp, Str),
        asserta(pp_reg(Str)),          /* store PP */
        check_build(vp2, Sb).

    transition(s6, Sa, Sb):-
        check_PP(pp, Sa, Sb),
        trace(on),
        build_phrase(pp, Str),         /* store PP */
        asserta(pp_reg(Str)),
        build_phrase(vp2, Str1),
        asserta(vp_reg(Str1)),         /* store verb */
        set_state(s7).
```

```
/******************************************************************/
/* Noun phrase transitions    */

    transition(np, Sa, Sb):-
        get_token(Sa, W, Sb),
        word_type(W, det),
        asserta(det_reg(W)),           /* store dterminer */
        asserta(adj_reg("")),
        set_state(np1).

    transition(np, Sa, Sb):-
        get_token(Sa, W, Sb),
        word_type(W, noun),
        asserta(noun_reg(W)),          /* store noun */
        asserta(adj_reg("")),
        set_state(np3).

    transition(np, Sa, Sb):-
        get_token(Sa, W, Sb),
        word_type(W, pronoun),
        asserta(noun_reg(W)),          /* store noun */
        asserta(adj_reg("")),
        set_state(np3).

    transition(np1, Sa, Sb):-
        get_token(Sa, W, Sb),
        word_type(W, noun),
        asserta(noun_reg(W)),          /* store noun */
        set_state(np2).

    transition(np1, Sa, Sb):-
        get_token(Sa, W, Sb),
        word_type(W, adj),
        adj_reg(Adjr),
        concat(Adjr, " ", A1),
        concat(A1, W, A2),
        asserta(adj_reg(A2)).          /* store adjective */
```

```
/******************************************************************/
/*    Prepositional phrase transitions        */
      transition(pp, Sa, Sb):-
         get_token(Sa, W, Sb),
         word_type(W, prep),
         asserta(prep_reg(W)),              /* store preposition */
         set_state(pp1).

      transition(pp1, Sa, Sb):-
         check_NP(np, Sa, Sb),
         build_phrase(np, Str),
         asserta(np_reg(Str)),              /* store noun phrase */
         set_state(pp2).

/******************************************************************/
/*    NP RTN      */
      check_NP(np2, Sc, Sb):- Sb = Sc, !.

      check_NP(np3, Sc, Sb):- Sb = Sc, !.

      check_NP(St, Sa, Sb):-
         transition(St, Sa, Sc),
         get_state(Ns),
         check_NP(Ns, Sc, Sb), !.

/******************************************************************/
/*  PP RTN          */
      check_PP(pp2, Sc, Sb):- Sb = Sc, !.

      check_PP(St, Sa, Sb):-
         transition(St, Sa, Sc),
         get_state(Ns),
         check_PP(Ns, Sc, Sb), !.

/******************************************************************/
/* Build Phrases */
      build_phrase(np, Str):-
         det_reg(Detr),
         adj_reg(Adjr),
         noun_reg(Nounr),
         get_template(np,T),
         fill_template(T, Detr, T1),
         fill_template(T1, Adjr, T2),
         fill_template(T2, Nounr, Str).

      build_phrase(vp1, Str):-
         aux_reg(Auxr),
         verb_reg(Verbr),
         get_template(vp, T),
         fill_template(T, Auxr, T1),
         fill_template(T1, Verbr, Str).
```

(continued)

```
      build_phrase(vp2, Str):-
        aux_reg(Auxr),
        verb_reg(Verbr),
        obj_reg(Objr),
        pp_reg(Ppr),
        get_template(vp, T),
        fill_template(T, Auxr, T1),
        fill_template(T1, Verbr, T2),
        fill_template(T2, Objr, T3),
        fill_template(T3, Ppr, Str).

      build_phrase(pp, Str):-
        prep_reg(Prepr),
        np_reg(Npr),
        get_template(pp, T),
        fill_template(T, Prepr, T1),
        fill_template(T1, Npr, Str).

      build_phrase(s, Str):-
        type_reg(Typr),
        subj_reg(Subjr),
        vp_reg(Vpr),
        get_template(s, T),
        fill_template(T, Typr, T1),
        fill_template(T1, Subjr, T2),
        fill_template(T2, Vpr, Str).

      build_phrase(s1, Str):-
        type_reg(Typr),
        vp_reg(Vpr),
        get_template(s, T),
        fill_template(T, Typr, T1),
        fill_template(T1, Vpr, Str).

      check_build(Type, S):-
        S = ".",
        build_phrase(Type, Str),
        asserta(vp_reg(Str)).

      check_build(_,_).



/****************************************************************/
/*** Phrase Templates  ***/

      get_template(np, "[NP]").
      get_template(vp, "[VP]").
```

```
    get_template(pp, "[PP]").
    get_template(s, "[]").

    fill_template(T, Str, Result):-
       Str= "",
       Result = T.

    fill_template(T, Str, Result):-
       trace(off),
       strclfind(T, ']', P),
       strsi(T, " ", P, T1),
       Pos = P + 1,
       strsi(T1, Str, Pos, Result),
       trace(on).
```

```
/*+++++++++++++++++++++++++++++++++++++++++++++++++++++++++++++++ */
```

```
/*    words....     */
    word_type("a", det).
    word_type("the", det).
    word_type("that", det).
    word_type("I", pronoun).
    word_type("you", pronoun).
    word_type("files", noun).
    word_type("disk", noun).
    word_type("boy", noun).
    word_type("newspaper", noun).
    word_type("computer", noun).
    word_type("book", noun).
    word_type("magazine", noun).
    word_type("table", noun).
    word_type("can", aux).
    word_type("will", aux).
    word_type("is", verb).
    word_type("are", verb).
    word_type("reads", verb).
    word_type("programs", verb).
    word_type("run", verb).
    word_type("execute", verb).
    word_type("on", prep).
    word_type("at", prep).
    word_type("in", prep).
    word_type("hard", adj).
    word_type("big", adj).
    word_type("happy", adj).
```

Notes on the ATN

As you probably have noticed, the ATN parser is much more powerful than the RTN developed earlier. The ATN not only can analyze a sentence to determine if it is grammatical but can also build the structure of a sentence. The advantage of the ATN over the RTN is that the structural information created by the ATN analysis can be used later on for further analysis. Of course, the ATN does not provide a very in-depth analysis of the meaning or semantics of a sentence. Although ATN's have their limitations, they can be very useful for building programs such as natural language query systems.

The ATN developed in this section is also limited because of its small vocabulary. If you want to extend the capabilities of the ATN, you could easily add more words to the database. Of course, as the the program grows in size and complexity, you would want to compile it and run it as a stand-alone program.

CHAPTER 6

Knowledge Representation

To create programs that have "intelligent" qualities, it is necessary to develop techniques for representing knowledge. Unlike people, computers do not have the ability to acquire knowledge on their own. Any knowledge they contain about the world has been explicitly provided in the form of data and knowledge structures. In the previous chapter, the natural language processing programs were limited because they did not contain knowledge about the meaning of the words used in a sentence. If you provided the following sentence to one of the transition networks:

```
Veronica writes programs at the computer.
```

the program would not have any idea who Veronica is or what kind of computer she is working on. The program only contains knowledge about the syntax, or proper ordering of words in a sentence.

AI programs depend heavily on the representation of the types of knowledge that people use to solve complex tasks. In this chapter some of the important techniques for representing knowledge in a program are presented. The techniques vary from simple representations such as facts to complex knowledge structures. Fortunately, Turbo Prolog provides some useful facilities for developing techniques for knowledge representation.

The Traditional Approach

Traditional programs use data structures to store information. If you have had experience programming in a high level language such as Pascal or C, you are probably familiar with such data structures as arrays, records, or structures. These data structures are very useful for storing certain types of data; however, if you need to represent the kinds of complex relationships found in a AI program such as an expert system, you might discover that these data structures are limited. To improve the performance of AI programs, researchers and software developers have been working for many years to come up with better techniques for storing and using knowledge.

The AI Approach

AI programs use structures called knowledge structures to represent objects, facts, rules, relationships, and procedures. The main function of the knowledge structure is to provide the needed expertise and information so that a program can operate in an intelligent manner. Knowledge structures are usually composed of both traditional data structures and other complex structures such as frames, scripts, and semantic networks which will be discussed in this chapter. Knowledge structures are usually closely tailored to specific problem areas which are called problem domains. The domain is the set of relevant information required to solve a specific problem. For example, if you were interested in writing a program to play expert level chess, your domain would consist of the rules and facts needed to play the game as well as the strategic information needed to play well enough to beat an expert. Your domain would not include information such as the color of the player's hair or the name of the 12th President of the United States because this information is not directly relevant to the game.

Another useful tool for the AI programmer is the concept of the knowledge base. A knowledge base is a special type of database which holds the specific information (knowledge) about a subject. In Chapter 4, the inference engine you built used a simple knowledge base which contained the facts for diagnosing a computer/printer problem.

There are many techniques for representing knowledge in a knowledge base, however, most techniques involve some type of system of classification. For example, if you needed to create a knowledge base to be used in a program for weather prediction, you could divide the knowledge into three categories: conclusions, questions, and rules. The definitions of these catagories might be:

Conclusions. This category contains the possible conclusions or outcomes that can be derived from the known facts stored in the knowledge base. Some sample conclusions might be:

```
The forecast is for afternoon precipitation.
The forecast is for blizzard conditions.
```

Questions. This category defines the specific questions and the possible answers associated with each question. Here is an example:

```
What type of cloud cover is there today?
Acceptable answers: stratus, nimbocumulus, cumulus.
```

Rules. This category contains the representation of the logical decisions used to reach conclusions. The basic structure of these rules are usually:

```
IF <condition> THEN <conclusion>
```

An example:

```
IF Little or no cloud cover
AND Today's temperature is > 90 degrees
AND The season is Summer
THEN The forecast is for afternoon precipitation.
```

Knowledge Bases vs. Databases

Although knowledge bases share some of the functions found in database management systems such as storing and retrieving information, they are much more powerful. The structure of data storage in most conventional database systems is usually flat, unlike knowledge bases which organize knowledge in hierarchical structures. Data in traditional database systems is stored in units called records. Figures 6.1 and 6.2 illustrate how a conventional database management system might store information about types of cars. In Figure 6.1, the major category "car" is divided into a number of data items. The classification of "sports car" or "station wagon" can be created by adding another field. This requires that all data items be checked each time you search for "sports car"—an operation which is extremely inefficient if the database is large. To improve this inefficiency, you might create separate databases as shown in Figure 6.2. This change simplifies the search for the sports car category but now it would be difficult to obtain a list of all the cars—each database would have to be searched. If new categories such as "sub-compacts" or "four-doors" were added, then the program must be modified to search these new areas. In summary, the database management systems are not able to handle the hierarchical information necessary to fully describe the relationships between the various categories.

In the knowledge based system, the hierarchy and the data are all part of the same structure. One type of knowledge representation uses a concept called frames to represent the hierarchical structure and a concept called instances to repre-

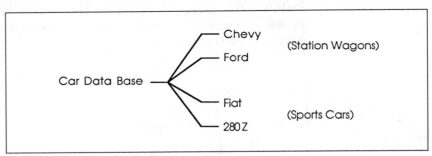

Figure 6.1 Organization of a Simple Database

sent the actual knowledge. As shown in Figure 6.3, the frame "car" consists of the frames "sports car" and "station wagon." These frames each have the instances or actual names of specific cars. Frames and instances will both be covered in greater detail later in this chapter.

The data retrieval features in a knowledge base system are also more powerful than those found in database systems. In a database management system, only the data that is already stored in the database can be retrieved. In a knowledge based system, information or knowledge can be inferred from the data already in the system.

In summary, database management systems are a collection of data that represent facts. The volume of data can be quite large and it changes often. The correctness of the data is determined by comparing it with its source, such as the real world. The data can be entered by anyone without any special training in the specific area. The knowledge base, on the other hand, is developed by or in cooperation with the experts that have knowledge or expertise about the subject. It contains facts as well as the high level knowledge structures.

Types of Knowledge Represented in a Program

No one really knows exactly how the human brain stores knowledge, therefore it is difficult to come up with the ideal knowledge representation to enable a computer to simulate intelligent behavior. Nevertheless, AI researchers have found it useful to define classifications for the types of knowledge that people use.

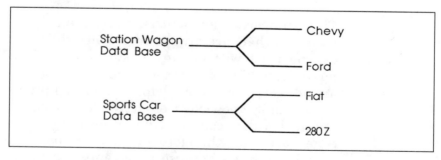

Figure 6.2   Improvement of the Car Database

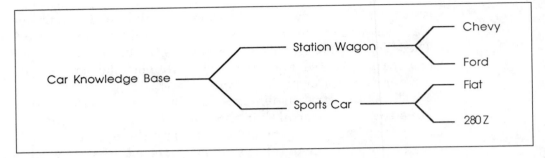

Figure 6.3   Representing Knowledge with Frames

Some of the important areas are:

- Static Knowledge
- Dynamic or Active Knowledge
- Surface Knowledge
- Deep Knowledge
- Heuristic Knowledge
- Procedural Knowledge
- Declarative Knowledge

Static knowledge is the type of knowledge which does not change during the life of a program. This knowledge is the easiest to work with because you only have to represent it once. For example, if you wanted to express some of the characteristics that exist between simple geometric objects, you could easily represent this in Turbo Prolog as:

```
round(circle).
square(box).
curve(arc).
```

These properties are written as facts and they express relationships that are always true. Once they are defined, they can be used without any modifications. Static knowledge, however, is limited. Programs that only use static knowledge are not very useful for solving complex AI problems.

Dynamic knowledge or active knowledge is the type of knowledge that can be acquired over time. Dynamic knowledge bases are therefore much more powerful than static knowledge bases because they can grow and change during the execution of a program. Dynamic knowledge is especially necessary for learning programs. As an example of how dynamic knowledge can be represented in a program, assume you wanted to store the facts about the state of road conditions during the evening rush hour commute. You could create the necessary representation with Turbo Prolog's database clause:

```
database
    traffic_jam(symbol)
    collision(symbol)
```

Now with this structure, you could add dynamic knowledge by asserting facts with these predicates. For example, the statements:

```
assert(traffic_jam(elm_street)).
assert(collision(first_ave)).
```

would add the necessary knowledge. You could also obtain knowledge at any time by using the built-in retract clause. The statement:

```
retract(traffic_jam(X)).
```

would return the appropriate fact. Of course, this clause would also remove the knowledge from the knowledge base. To perform a simple lookup you could write:

```
traffic_jam(X).
```

If you wanted to change the knowledge, you could retract the old knowledge and use the assert statement to add new knowledge at any time during the life of the program.

Surface knowledge is the the basic "rule-of-thumb" knowledge that people accumulate through experiences. As the name implies, this knowledge is based on the more superficial aspects of a specific topic. Deep knowledge, on the other hand, is knowledge which is based on the theories, facts, and principles related to a specific topic. In one sense, you could consider surface knowledge to serve as the outline of a problem and deep knowledge to serve as the details. Both types of knowledge typically are used by people for problem solving activities.

As an example, assume you are interested in learning how to perform magic. You might first go and watch a magician perform in order to learn some of the basics. At this point, you are acquiring surface knowledge. This knowledge is based on observation. With this knowledge, you might try to perform some of the magic you saw the magician perform; however, you probably won't get very far. You are lacking the deeper knowledge, or principles that the magician has. In order to perform well, you would need to study the theories of magic with an expert.

Heuri. tic knowledge is the type of knowledge that has a built-in hierarchical or top-down order. Heuristic knowledge is usually represented graphically with the inverted tree structure. As an example, consider the knowledge that a company manager might use to determine if an employee should be given a raise. This knowledge can be represented in what is commonly called a decision tree as shown in Figure 6.4. With heuristic knowledge, it is important that a certain order is maintained in the knowledge structure. The interrelationships between knowledge in a heuristic knowledge structure is important.

Procedural knowledge is knowledge that can be represented as a procedure or process. In computer programs, this

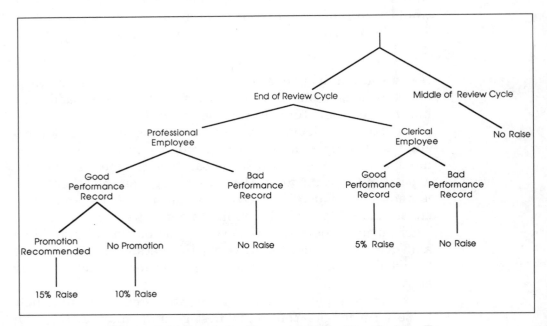

Figure 6.4 Knowledge Representation with a Decision Tree

type of knowledge is stored as code, not data. Most programming algorithms are a form of procedural knowledge because they contain the information about how to perform a specific task. In fact, most tasks that require a step-by-step approach use procedural knowledge. For example, consider the procedure for sorting a list of company addresses by zip code. The process would involve comparing two addresses at a time and placing the lowest zip code address at the top of the list. This approach to representing knowledge is easy to work with if the problem you are trying to solve can be described procedurally.

Declarative knowledge, on the other hand, is knowledge which can be stored as data. The important aspect about declarative knowledge is that it can be stored separately from program code. Of course, knowledge structures such as facts and rules are examples of declarative knowledge. For many types of AI programs, the declarative approach is well suited for representing knowledge about objects, relationships, and events.

Keep in mind, however, that using only a declarative or procedural representation in a program is not enough to provide you with the flexibility needed to create intelligent programs. Each one, however, has its advantages. With a declarative representation, it is easy to add or modify knowledge because the knowledge is independent of the program itself. Declarative knowledge is also easier to read and maintain. On the other hand, procedural knowledge is better suited for tasks that can easily be described by procedures. In most knowledge based systems in use today, both procedural and declarative approaches are used.

Turbo Prolog's Knowledge Representation Capabilities

The field of knowledge representation is one of the most important areas of artificial intelligence research. Researchers have spent many years developing and experimenting with different types of programming languages in their quest to develop better representations of knowledge. In order to represent knowledge easily and accurately, it is important to have a programming language that is flexible enough to accommodate complex relationships and situations. In reality, almost any language could be used; however, a language such as Turbo Prolog has many benefits because of both its declarative and procedural nature. Do not be misled by thinking that Turbo Prolog is only a declarative language and it therefore cannot be used to represent procedural knowledge.

In attempting to represent knowledge in a computer program, one of the first questions that must be addressed is: How should the knowledge be represented? To help you answer this question, the following sections provide a discussion of some of the more interesting and useful techniques for representing knowledge.

Knowledge Representation with Logic

The predicate logic introduced in Chapter 4 is one useful form of knowledge representation. Such predicates can be used to represent facts about the world. For example, the predicates:

```
owns(john, sports_car).
fast(sports_car).
```

contain the facts: John owns a sports car and sports cars are fast.

Such knowledge is considered to be partial knowledge because only the information that is directly defined is available for solving problems. Undefined conditions or incomplete knowledge could not be represented easily with such simple logic. If conditions change, modifications to the knowledge base such as insertions or deletions of predicates would be necessary. Therefore, the primary drawback to this representation scheme is its use of large amounts of memory. Every fact must be uniquely defined.

Using Turbo Prolog to solve a simple problem will help you understand how logic can be used as a technique for knowledge representation. Consider the classic farmer problem. The farmer has a sheep, a wolf, and a head of cabbage that must be transported from the west side of a river to the east side. He also has a boat; however, due to new government regulations, he can only take one passenger at a time. The government regulations also state that all objects must be considered passengers, therefore the cabbage must be treated as a passenger. To further complicate matters, the sheep can't be left alone with the wolf because the wolf will eat the sheep and the sheep can't be left with the cabbage because the sheep will eat the cabbage.

To solve the problem, you can consider each item as an object, thus there are four objects: farmer, sheep, fox, and cabbage. The arrangement of these objects constitute a state. Therefore, the current status of the problem can be defined by the state of the objects (where the objects are in relation to each other and the banks of the river). A state can be expressed as:

```
state(Farmer, Wolf, Sheep, Cabbage).
```

where the terms "Farmer," "Wolf," "Sheep," and "Cabbage" represent variables that can be assigned a value "east" or "west." Keep in mind that the exact order of these variables is not important but, once chosen, the order must be maintained. After defining the problem, it is now necessary to select the boundary conditions or states:

```
initial state:   state(west, east, west, west)
final state:     state(east, east, east, east)
```

Finally, to solve the problem, you must build a knowledge base of the known facts and relations. For example, if the farmer or one of the other passengers change sides, it is necessary to represent this information. To indicate this, the terms "east" and "west" are used. The predicate which defines the relationship between the four objects is:

```
state(Old_side, Old_side, Sheep, Cabbage) :-
    swap_sides(New_side, Old_side),
    state(New_side, New_side, Sheep, Cabbage).

    swap_sides(east, west).
    swap_sides(west, east).
```

In this case, the farmer and the wolf are initially on the same side. When they change sides, a recursive call to the "state" clause is initiated to look for the next move. This clause calls "swap_sides" which performs the task of switching sides from east to west or west to east.

The rules which describe the arrangement of the objects are defined with the following predicates:

```
allowed(Farmer, Wolf, Sheep, Cabbage) :-
      ok(Sheep, Wolf, Farmer),
      ok(Sheep, Cabbage, Farmer).

ok(Same_side, Same_side, Same_side).
ok(Sheep, Object1, _) :-
      swap_sides(Sheep, Object1).
```

The predicate "allowed" determines if the move is legal by checking for an invalid situation. If the sheep is not in danger from the wolf and the cabbage is not in danger from the sheep, then this predicate succeeds. The second predicate, "ok," determines which pair is with the farmer: the wolf and the sheep or the sheep and the cabbage. If one of these pairs is not with the farmer, then each member must be on opposite sides of the river. For example, if the wolf and the sheep are not with the farmer, then the sheep must be on one side of the river and the wolf must be on the other side.

In this program, the same state could be revisited because of Turbo Prolog's backtracking scheme. To eliminate the possibility of creating an infinite loop, an assert of "save_state" is used to keep track of the states that have already been reached. The database definition for "save_state" is:

```
database
      save_state(symbol, symbol, symbol, symbol)
```

and the change to the "state" predicate is:

```
state( Old_side, Old_side, Sheep, Cabbage ) :-
   swap_sides( New_side, Old_side ),
   allowed( New_side, New_side, Sheep, Cabbage ),
   not( save_state( New_side, New_side, Sheep,
         Cabbage )),
   asserta( save_state( Old_side, Old_side, Sheep,
         Cabbage )),
   state( New_side, New_side, Sheep, Cabbage),
   write( New_side, " ", New_side, " ", Sheep, " ",
         Cabbage ),

   nl.
```

The complete program is shown here:

Listing 6.1

```
/*    Logic Programming */

/*    initial state:    state( west, west, west, west ).
      final state:      state( east, east, east, east ).  */
database

    save_state( symbol, symbol, symbol, symbol )

predicates

    allowed(symbol, symbol, symbol, symbol)
    ok( symbol, symbol, symbol )
    run()
    state( symbol, symbol, symbol, symbol )
    swap_sides( symbol, symbol )

clauses

    run() :- retract( save_state( _, _, _, _ )), fail.
    run() :- assert( save_state( east, east, east, east )),
        state( east, east, east, east ),
        write( "east   east  east   east" ), nl.


    state( west, west, west, west ) :-        /* Initial state */
        write( "\nFarmer Wolf  Sheep  Cabbage" ), nl.

    state( Old_side, Old_side, Sheep, Cabbage ) :-
        swap_sides( New_side, Old_side ),
        allowed( New_side, New_side, Sheep, Cabbage ),
        not( save_state( New_side, New_side, Sheep, Cabbage )),
        asserta( save_state( Old_side, Old_side, Sheep,
            Cabbage )),
        state( New_side, New_side, Sheep, Cabbage),
        write( New_side, "   ", New_side, " ", Sheep, "   ",
            Cabbage ),
        nl.

    state( Old_side, Wolf, Old_side, Cabbage ) :-
        swap_sides( New_side, Old_side ),
        allowed( New_side, Wolf, New_side, Cabbage ),
        not( save_state( New_side, Wolf, New_side, Cabbage )),
        asserta( save_state( Old_side, Wolf, Old_side,
            Cabbage )),
        state( New_side, Wolf, New_side, Cabbage),
```

(continued)

```
write( New_side, "    ", Wolf, "  ", New_side, "    ",
    Cabbage ),
nl.

state( Old_side, Wolf, Sheep, Old_side ) :-
    swap_sides( New_side, Old_side ),
    not( save_state( New_side, Wolf, Sheep, New_side )),
    allowed( New_side, Wolf, Sheep, New_side ),
    asserta( save_state( Old_side, Wolf, Sheep, Old_side )),
    state( New_side, Wolf, Sheep, New_side),
    write( New_side, "  ", Wolf, "  ", Sheep, "    ",
        New_side ),
    nl.

state( Old_side, Wolf, Sheep, Cabbage ) :-
    swap_sides( New_side, Old_side ),
    allowed( New_side, Wolf, Sheep, Cabbage ),
    not( save_state( New_side, Wolf, Sheep, Cabbage )),
    asserta( save_state( Old_side, Wolf, Sheep, Cabbage )),
    state( New_side, Wolf, Sheep, Cabbage),
    write( New_side, "  ", Wolf, "  ", Sheep, "    ",
        Cabbage ),
    nl.

allowed( Farmer, Wolf, Sheep, Cabbage ) :-
    ok( Sheep, Wolf, Farmer ),
    ok( Sheep, Cabbage, Farmer ).

ok( Same_side, Same_side, Same_side ).
ok( Sheep, Object1, _ ) :-
    swap_sides( Sheep, Object1 ).

swap_sides( east, west ).
swap_sides( west, east ).
```

Knowledge Representation with Frames

One useful concept for representing knowledge developed by the well known AI researcher, Marvin Minsky, is called frames. The frames concept consists of dividing knowledge up into specified categories. Frames function like tables or questionnaires. They are often implemented as table-like data structures in which all of the information in a given category is grouped together.

Like the entries in a table, frames can have numerous slots or places where information can be stored. For example, if you wanted to create a frame to represent a description of an airplane, you might have slots for such categories as color, length, engine type, wingspan, speed, etc. This example is shown in Figure 6.5.

Note the table-like characteristic of this frame. Another important feature provided with frames is the fact that the slots can have default values. This means that it is not necessary to describe in detail all of the facts about a given object. In the frame example of the airplane, you might create a frame with the defaults shown in Figure 6.6. These defaults will be used whenever the information for the slots in the airplane frame is omitted. The advantage of this frame representation is that it supports the situations where not all of the knowledge is available.

Since slots can reference other frames, often referred to as child frames, they are quite flexible. Therefore one frame can reference another frame which in turn can reference other frames. As an example of this feature, consider the problem of describing a computer system which consists of sub-systems such as keyboards, monitors, and peripherals. These sub-systems have their own additional sub-systems. For example, the peripheral sub-system has printer and plotter sub-systems. Here a frame can be used to specify each sub-system, with the slots in each frame describing that sub-system. For the printer, the slots can describe the type of interface, the width, and the type of paper feed.

Airplane Frame

Color	
Length	
Engine Type	
Wing Span	
Speed	
Weight	

Figure 6.5 Airplane Frame

This approach to knowledge representation is the basis for many sophisticated expert system development tools. Frames can be dynamically linked to other frames, thus representing the hierarchical knowledge about a problem. In addition, this approach provides the current status and progress toward reaching a solution. In our example, the basic computer configuration as well as the current configuration can be described.

Figure 6.7 contains the template of a frame which could be used by a computer diagnostic or configuration management

Airplane Frame

Color	White
Length	50 ft.
Engine Type	Volkswagen
Wing Span	75 ft.
Speed	100 mph
Weight	2000 lbs.

Figure 6.6 Airplane Frame with Knowledge

Knowledge Frame

Frame Title: _____
Frame Author: _____
Frame Usage: _____
Level: _____
Parent: _____
Comment: _____

SLOT NAME	UPPER RANGE	LOWER RANGE	LEGAL VALUES	DEFAULT VALUE	VALUE	COMMENT
____	____	____	____	____	____	____
____	____	____	____	____	____	____
____	____	____	____	____	____	____
____	____	____	____	____	____	____

Figure 6.7 Frame Template

system. It consists of fields for storing general information about the frame itself, such as title, author, and usage. The "parent" field contains the name of the frame that references this one. The level field indicates the level of hierarchy of this frame. In addition, each frame has slots. There is no limit to the number of slots that a frame can have. Slots can also have support fields or attributes. These fields help define and describe the value of the slot. For example, the limit for numeric slot values is given by the upper and lower range values. For non-numeric answers, the legal value attribute contains the list of possible candidates. The default value is the value used if no other explicit information is available.

This representation allows for more flexibility and greater accessibility to the knowledge. Frames are useful for handling complex structures. By assigning specific slots, the frame-processing system can recognize when there is information missing from the knowledge base and handle it as required. Simple frame systems can have a clear hierarchical structure similar to that of a tree data structure. Frames also simplify the addition of methods of handling default values for pieces of information not explicitly stated.

To help you understand the frame based knowledge representation, consider the hierarchy of the simple personal computer system previously discussed. The computer system is composed of a monitor, keyboard, peripherals, and internal sub-systems. The internal sub-systems consist of units such as a disc controller, extended memory, the cpu card, and so on. Likewise, the peripherals sub-system can be further partitioned into printer, plotter, and mouse. See Figure 6.8 for the basic hierarchical diagram of this computer system.

Building Frames with Turbo Prolog

Using the frame layout in Figure 6.8 as a guide, you are going to learn how to build a simple frame representation in this section. The first step is to determine the necessary storage format. One approach consists of using one large compound clause to create all of the frame and slot units. This approach uses memory efficiently because the data is kept in one memory location. Unfortunately, it is harder to maintain and understand. To simplify this example, two different clause formats are used: "frame_list" for storing frames and "slot_list"

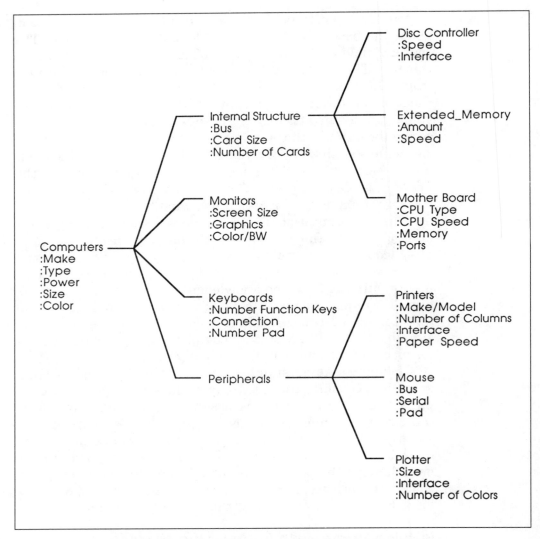

Figure 6.8   Hierarchical Representation of a Computer System

for storing slots. To begin this example, the clause for creating frames "new_frame" is discussed:

```
database
    frame_list( string, string, integer, string )

predicates
    new_frame( string, string, string )
```

```
clauses
   new_frame( F_name, _, _ ) :-
         frame_list( F_name, _, _, _ ),
         write( "\nError - Frame: ", F_name,
            " Already Exists." ).

   new_frame( F_name, Par_name, Comment ) :-
         frame_list( Par_name, _, Top_level, _ ),
         F_level = Top_level + 1,
         assertz( frame_list( F_name, Par_name,
         F_level,Comment )).

   new_frame( F_name, _, _ ) :-
            write( "\nError - Possibly invalid Parent
               Name: ", F_name ).
```

The arguments for this clause are the frame name, the parents frame name, and the comment field which can be used to describe the author, use, or other information about the frame. The comment field is used as an aid for maintaining the knowledge base. The parents frame name provides a backward link to the previous frame, thus creating a hierarchical structure for the knowledge. "New_frame" first verifies that the frame doesn't already exist. Initially, the second "new_frame" clause verifies that the parent frame exists and then it increments the frame level. This information is used to assert the new frame. The last "new_frame" is only called if the parent frame doesn't exist. If it is called, it outputs an error message. The following statements demonstrate the use of the "new_frame" clause:

```
new_frame( computers, top, "Top level of hierarchy" ).
new_frame( monitors, computers, "CRT Screen" ).
new_frame( peripherals, computers, "There are many." ).
new_frame( mouse, peripherals, "Not on all systems." ).
```

The first statement creates a frame called "computers." This frame is the top level frame; its parents names is "top." The comment argument is used to store a note about this frame.

To support the frame structure, the following two clauses are developed. One initializes the knowledge base while the other lists the current structure:

```
predicates
   init()
   list( symbol )
```

```
clauses
 init() :-
     retract( frame_list( _, _, _, _ )),
     fail.
 init() :-
     assertz( frame_list( top, myself, 0,
             Top of Structure" )).
 list( frames ) :-
     makewindow( 1, 1, 7, "FRAME LIST", 1, 1, 20, 6 ),
     write( "\nFrame\t\tParent\t\tLevel" ),
     frame_list( F_name, Par_name, F_level, _ ),
     write( "\n", F_name, "\t", Par_name, "\t",
     F_level ),
     fail.
 list( frames ) :- nl,
      write( "\nPress any key to continue." ),
     readchar( _ ).
```

The "init" clause removes the old frames and asserts a special "end-of-structure" frame. This first frame represents the top of the frame hierarchy. All other frames are linked directly or indirectly to this frame. The "fail" predicate in the first "init" clause forces the current "init" clause to fail and causes the next "init" clause to be executed. When the other "init" clause is added for removing the slot storage, it must be inserted before the "init" clause with an assert.

The "list" clause is a tool for displaying all currently defined frames. Here a window is opened and a column heading is displayed. Each frame is then displayed along with the name of its parent and its frame level. After all frames have been displayed, the clause fails causing the last "list" clauses to be initiated. Pressing any key causes the window to be closed. Similar "list (Argument)" clauses are going to be added as this example progresses. The Argument specifies whether slots, values, or comments are displayed.

Now that you have seen how to add frames in a hierarchical structure, you are ready to examine the slot storage structure. Here is the code:

```
domains
    slist = symbol*
    vlist = string*
database
     slot_list( string, string, symbol, integer,
```

```
        integer,
            vlist, string, string, string )
```

The "slot_list" clause is a structure containing a number of arguments such as the frame name, the slot name, the slot value, and comments. The comment argument serves the same purpose as the one found in the "new_frame" clause. In this example, there are four types of slot values: open, frame, integer, and symbol. One of these is stored as the slot type. An integer slot type indicates that a new slot value must be compared with the upper and lower limits specified for that slot. For a slot type of symbol, the "legal_val" argument contains a list of the candidate slot values. These are the only values that this slot is allowed to handle. The open slot type has no restrictions so that any value can be placed in this type of slot. The last slot type is the frame which allows the slot to point to another frame. This provides a forward link structure for the knowledge base:

```
predicates
        member( string, vlist )
        member( symbol, slist )
        new_slot( string, string, symbol, integer, integer
                vlist, string, string )
        slot_type( symbol )


database
        slot_list( string, string, symbol, integer, integer,
            vlist, string, string, string )


predicates
        new_slot( string, string, symbol, integer, integer,
            vlist, string, string )


clauses
        new_slot( F_name, S_name, _, _, _, _, _, _ ) :-
            slot_list( F_name, S_name, _, _, _, _,_,_,- ),
                write( "\nError - Slot: ", S_name, " Already Exists ",
                "In This Frame: ", F_name ).

        new_slot( F_name, S_name, S_type, Up_val, Low_val,
            Legal_val, Default, Comment ) :-
                frame_list( F_name, _, _, _ ), !,
```

```
        slot_type( S_type ),
        assertz( slot_list( F_name, S_name, S_type, Up_val,
            Low_val, Legal_val, Default, Default, Comment )).


new_slot( F_name, _, _, _, _, _, _, _ ) :-
    write( "\nError - Frame: ", F_name,
        "Does Not Exist." ).


slot_types( S_type ) :-
    member( S_type, [ open, frame, integer, symbol ] ).


slot_types( S_type ) :-
    write( "\nError - Invalid slot type: ", S_type ),
    fail.


member( Value, [ Value: _ ] ).


member( Value, [ _ | Rest ] ) :- !,
    member(Value, Rest ).
```

Before inserting a new slot, the first "new_slot" clause checks to be sure that the frame and slot don't already exist. Because it checks for the specified frame along with the slot, the ability to add the same slot name to different frames is still available. If this is a unique slot, then the next "new_slot" clause checks to verify that the specified frame does exists. If not, then the second clause fails and the third clause displays an error message.

If the frame exists, then the second "new_slot" clause causes the "slot_types" clause to be initiated. This clause determines if the specified slot type is valid. If the slot type is valid, then the "slot_list" clause is asserted. If it isn't, then an error message is displayed and the "slot_type" clause fails.

Note that in "new_slot," a cut operator is placed after the "frame_list" clause. This cut operator prevents the failure of the "slot_type" clause from causing the backtracking of the "new_slot" clause. If it did backtrack, the third "new_slot" clause would display an extra error message.

Each slot contains a default value. As mentioned earlier, one of the powerful features of the frame knowledge representation is its ability to provide knowledge for the areas in which the knowledge is missing or incomplete. The following examples demonstrate the use of the "new_slot" clause:

```
new_slot(keyboards, function_keys, integer, 32, 0, [],
  "16", "Number of Function Keys").
new_slot(keyboards, number_pad, symbol, 0, 0, [yes, no],
  yes, "Is there one?").
new_slot(printers, make_model, open, 0, 0, [],
  toshiba_1350, "What make and model?").
new_slot(peripherals, printer_slot, frame, 0, 0, [],
  "", "Name of frame for this slot.").
```

Now that the slots have been defined, the feature must be added to allow you to enter or change slot values. Because there are four types of slots, four clauses, one for each type must be added. Here are the clauses for changing slot values:

```
predicates
    new_slot_value( string, string, string )
    new_slot_value_1( symbol, string, string, string )

clauses
    new_slot_value( F_name, S_name, Value ) :-
        slot_list( F_name, S_name, S_type, _, _, _, _, _, _ ),
        new_slot_value_1( S_type, F_name, S_name, Value ).

    new_slot_value( F_name, S_name, _ ) :-
        write( :\nError - Frame: ", F_name, " or slot: ",
            S_name, " Does Not Exists." ).

    new_slot_value_1( open, F_name, S_name, Value ) :-
        slot_list( F_name, S_name, S_type, Up_val, Low_val,
            Legal_val, Default, _, Comment ),
        retract( slot_list( F_name, S_name, S_type, _, _, _, _, _, _ )),
        assertz( slot_list( F_name, S_name, S_type, Up_val,
            Low_val, Legal_val, Default, Value, Comment )

    new_slot_value_1( integer, F_name, S_name, Value ):-
        slot_list( F_name, S_name, S_type, Up_val, Low_val,
            Legal_val, Default, _, Comment ),
        str_int( Value, Int_value
        Int_value >= Low_val,
        Int_value <= Up_val,
```

```
    retract( slot_list( F_name, S_name, S_type, _, _, _, _, _, _ )),
    assertz( slot_list( F_name, S_name, S_type, Up_val,
        Low_val, Legal_val, Default, Value, Comment )).

new_slot_value_1( symbol, F_name, S_name, Value ) :-
    slot_list( F_name, S_name, S_type, Up_val, Low_val,
        Legal_val, Default, _, Comment ),
    member( Value, Legal_val ),
    retract( slot_list( F_name, S_name, S_type, _, _, _, _, _, _ )),
    assertz( slot_list( F_name, S_name, S_type, Up_val,
        Low_val, Legal_val, Default, Value, Comment )).

new_slot_value_1( frame, F_name, S_name, Value ) :-
    slot_list( F_name, S_name, S_type, Up_val, Low_val,
        Legal_val, Default, _, Comment ),
    frame_list( Value, _, _, _ ),
    retract( slot_list( F_name, S_name, S_type, _, _, _, _, _, _ )),
    assertz( slot_list( F_name, S_name, S_type, Up_val,
        Low_val, Legal_val, Default, Value, Comment )).
new_slot_value_1( _, F_name, S_name, Value ) :-
    write( "\nError - Invalid value: ", Value, " For ",
        "frame: ", F_name, ", And Slot: ", S_name ), nl.
```

The first "new_slot_value" clause determines if the frame and slot exist. If not, then an error message is displayed and the clause is aborted. If the slot does exist, then the slot type is determined and "new_slot_value_1" is initiated. Depending on the slot type, one of the four "new_slot_value_1" clauses is used. The first argument of the "new_slot_value_1" clause is matched with the appropriate slot type.

The integer version verifies that the new value is within the range specified by the upper and lower limits. The symbol version uses the "member" clauses to verify that the value is one of those specified by the list of legal values. The frame type determines if the value is the name of a valid frame type. If any errors are detected then this clause fails and the last "new_slot_value" is used to display an error message. The clause that processes the open slot type has no error checks so it asserts its data. Some sample "new_slot_values" are:

```
new_slot_value( keyboards, function_keys, "24" ).
new_slot_value( keyboards, connection, "direct" ).
new_slot_value( keyboards, number_pad, "no" ).
```

```
new_slot_value( peripherals, printer_slot, "printers" ),
new_slot_value( printers, make_model, "Okidata" ).
```

Now that you can define slots, the next step is to learn how information is retrieved from the slots. "Get_slot_value" returns the value of the slot with the specified frame and slot name. This clause first determines if the frame and slot exist. If they do exist then the current slot value is returned. If they don't exist, then an error message is displayed. Here is the code for "get_slot_value":

```
predicates
    get_slot_value( frame_name, slot_name, value )

clauses·
    get_slot_value( F_name, S_name, Value ) :-
        slot_list( F_name, S_name, _, _, _, _, _, Value,
            _ ), !.
    get_slot_value( F_name, S_name, "" ) :-
        write( "\nError - Frame: ", F_name, " And Slot:
        ", S_name, " Do Not Exist.\n" ).
```

Finally, there are two clauses needed to support the frame representation. "Delete_slot" uses the same techniques you've seen to verify that the slot and frame exist before retracting the slot. The "help" clause summarizes the options that are available for the frame knowledge representation.

The entire program is as follows:

Listing 6.2

```
/* Frame System */

domains

    slist = symbol*
    vlist = string*

database

    frame_list( string, string, integer, string )
    slot_list( string, string, symbol, integer, integer,
        vlist, string, string, string )
```

(continued)

```
predicates
    delete_slot( string, string )
    get_slot_value( string, string, string )
    help()
    init()
    list( symbol )
    member( string, vlist )
    member( symbol, slist )
    new_frame( string, string, string )
    new_slot( string, string, symbol, integer, integer,
        vlist, string, string )
    new_slot_value( string, string, string )
    new_slot_value_1( symbol, string, string, string )
    slot_type( symbol )

clauses
    init() :-
        retract( frame_list( _, _, _, _ )),
        fail.

    init() :-
        retract( slot_list( _, _, _, _, _, _, _, _, _ )),
        fail.

    init() :-
        assertz( frame_list( top, myself, 0,
            "Top of Structure" )).

    new_frame( F_name, _, _ ) :-
        frame_list( F_name, _, _, _ ),
        write( "\nError - Frame: ", F_name,
            " Already Exists." ).

    new_frame( F_name, Par_name, Comment ) :-
        frame_list( Par_name, _, Top_level, _ ),
        F_level = Top_level + 1,
        assertz( frame_list( F_name, Par_name, F_level, Comment )).

    new_frame( F_name, _, _ ) :-
        write( "\nError - Possibly invalid Parent Name: ",
            F_name ).

    new_slot( F_name, S_name, _, _, _, _, _, _ ) :-
        slot_list( F_name, S_name, _, _, _, _, _, _ ),
        write( "\nError - Slot: ", S_name, " Already Exists ",
            "In This Frame: ", F_name ).

    new_slot( F_name, S_name, S_type, Up_val, Low_val,
            Legal_val, Default, Comment ) :-
        frame_list( F_name, _, _, _ ), !,
        slot_types( S_type ),
        assertz( slot_list( F_name, S_name, S_type, Up_val,
            Low_val, Legal_val, Default, Default, Comment )).
```

```
new_slot( F_name, _, _, _, _, _, _, _ ) :-
    write( "\nError - Frame: ", F_name,
        " Does Not Exists." ).

new_slot_value( F_name, S_name, Value ) :-
    slot_list( F_name, S_name, S_type, _, _, _, _, _, _ ),
    new_slot_value_1( S_type, F_name, S_name, Value ).

new_slot_value( F_name, S_name, _ ) :-
    write( "\nError - Frame: ", F_name, " or slot: ",
        S_name, " Does Not Exists." ).

new_slot_value_1( open, F_name, S_name, Value ) :-
    slot_list( F_name, S_name, S_type, Up_val, Low_val,
        Legal_val, Default, _, Comment ),
    retract( slot_list( F_name, S_name, S_type, _, _, _
        _, _, _ )),
    assertz( slot_list( F_name, S_name, S_type, Up_val,
        Low_val, Legal_val, Default, Value, Comment )).

new_slot_value_1( integer, F_name, S_name, Value ) :-
    slot_list( F_name, S_name, S_type, Up_val, Low_val,
        Legal_val, Default, _, Comment ),
    str_int( Value, Int_value ),
    Int_value >= Low_val,
    Int_value <= Up_val,
    retract( slot_list( F_name, S_name, S_type, _, _, _
        _, _, _ )),
    assertz( slot_list( F_name, S_name, S_type, Up_val,
        Low_val, Legal_val, Default, Value, Comment )).

new_slot_value_1( symbol, F_name, S_name, Value ) :-
    slot_list( F_name, S_name, S_type, Up_val, Low_val,
        Legal_val, Default, _, Comment ),
    member( Value, Legal_val ),
    retract( slot_list( F_name, S_name, S_type, _, _, _
        _, _, _ )),
    assertz( slot_list( F_name, S_name, S_type, Up_val,
        Low_val, Legal_val, Default, Value, Comment )).

new_slot_value_1( frame, F_name, S_name, Value ) :-
    slot_list( F_name, S_name, S_type, Up_val, Low_val,
        Legal_val, Default, _, Comment ),
    frame_list( Value, _, _, _ ),
    retract( slot_list( F_name, S_name, S_type, _, _, _
        _, _, _ )),
    assertz( slot_list( F_name, S_name, S_type, Up_val,
        Low_val, Legal_val, Default, Value, Comment )).

new_slot_value_1( _, F_name, S_name, Value ) :-
    write( "\nError - Invalid value: ", Value, " For ",
        "frame: ", F_name, ", And Slot: ", S_name ), nl.
```

(continued)

```
slot_types( S_type ) :-
    member( S_type, [ open, frame, integer, symbol ] ).

slot_types( S_type ) :-
    write( "\nError - Invalid slot type: ", S_type ),
    fail.

get_slot_value( F_name, S_name, Value ) :-
    slot_list( F_name, S_name, _, _, _, _, _, Value, _ ), !.

get_slot_value( F_name, S_name, "" ) :-
    write( "\nError - Frame: ", F_name, " And Slot: ",
        S_name, " Do Not Exist.\n" ).

delete_slot( F_name, S_name ) :-
    slot_list( F_name, S_name, _, _, _, _, _, _, _ ),
    retract( slot_list( F_name, S_name, _, _, _, _,
        _, _, _ )).

delete_slot( F_name, S_name ) :-
    write( "\nError - Frame: ", F_name, " And Slot: ",
        S_name, " Do Not Exist." ).

member( Value, [ Value| _ ] ).

member( Value, [ _ | Rest ] ) :- !,
    member( Value, Rest ).

list( frames ) :-
    makewindow( 1, 1, 7, "FRAME LIST", 1, 1, 20, 60 ),
    write( "\nFrame\t\tParent\t\tLevel" ),
    frame_list( F_name, Par_name, F_level, _ ),
    write( "\n", F_name, "\t", Par_name, "\t", F_level ),
    fail.

list( frames ) :- nl,
    write( "\nPress any key to continue." ),
    readchar( _ ).

list( slots ) :-
    makewindow( 1, 1, 7, "SLOT LIST", 1, 1, 20, 79 ),
    write( "\nFrame\t\tSlot\t\tType\tUpper\tLower\t",
        "Default\tLegal" ),
    slot_list( F_name, S_name, S_type, Up_val, Low_val,
        Legal_val, Default, _, _ ),
    write( "\n", F_name, "\t", S_name, "\t", S_type, "\t",
        Up_val, "\t", Low_val, "\t", Default, "\t",
        Legal_val ),
    fail.

list( slots ) :- nl,
    write( "\nPress any key to continue." ),
    readchar( _ ).
```

```
list( values ) :-
    makewindow( 1, 1, 7, "SLOT VALUES", 1, 1, 20, 75 ),
    write( "\nFrame\t\tSlot\t\tValue" ),
    slot_list( F_name, S_name, _, _, _, _, _, Value, _ ),
    write( "\n", F_name, "\t", S_name, "\t", Value ),
    fail.

list( values ) :- nl,
    write( "\nPress any key to continue." ),
    readchar( _ ).

list( fcomments ) :-
    makewindow( 1, 1, 7, "FRAME COMMENTS", 1, 1, 20, 60 ),
    write( "\nFrame Name\tComment" ),
    frame_list( F_name, _, _, Comment ),
    write( "\n", F_name, "\t", Comment ),
    fail.

list( fcomments ) :- nl,
    write( "\nPress any key to continue." ),
    readchar( _ ).

list( scomments ) :-
    makewindow( 1, 1, 7, "SLOT COMMENTS", 1, 1, 20, 60 ),
    write( "\nFrame Name\tSlot Name\tComment" ),
    slot_list( F_name, S_name, _, _, _, _, _, _, Comment ),
    write( "\n", F_name, "\t", S_name, "\t", Comment ),
    fail.

list( scomments ) :- nl,
    write( "\nPress any key to continue." ),
    readchar( _ ).

help( ) :-
    makewindow( 1, 1, 7, "HELP INFORMATION", 1, 1, 20, 79 ),
    write( "\ninit - Clears old frames, set top frame." ),
    write( "\nhelp - This message." ),
    write( "\nlist( X ) - lists asserted values for X = ",
           "\n\tfcomments, scomments, frames, slots, ",
           "values." ),
    write( "\nload( X ) - load knowledge base X from",
           " f_data." ),

    write( "\nnew_frame( frame_name, parent_name,",
           " comment ) ",
           "- Create new frame." ),
    write( "\nnew_slot( frame_name, slot_name, slot_type, ",
           "upper_limit, lower_limit,\n\tlegal_values, ",
           "default, comment )",
           " - Create new slot." ),
```

(continued)

```
        write( "\nnew_slot_value( frame_name, slot_name, value",
             " ) - Change current slot value." ),
        write( "\nget_slot_value( frame_name, slot_name, value",
             " ) - Obtains slot value." ),
        write( "\ndelete_slot( frame_name, slot_name ) - ",
             "Delete slot." ),
        write( "\n\nPress any key to continue." ),
        readchar( _ ).

    include "f_data.pro"
```

The "include" predicate references a file which contains a subset of the data from Figure 6.8. This file uses a "load" predicate which executes a number of the clauses just defined, to build the framework for this simple knowledge base. Other knowledge bases could be placed in this file by using the same approach. These could then be loaded by using "load(symbol)" where symbol is the name referencing this other knowledge. The listing of this file is shown here:

```
/* Frame Data */

predicates

    load( symbol )

clauses

    load( computer ) :- init( ),
        new_frame( computers, top, "Top level of hierarchy." ),
        new_frame( intern_strs, computers,
            "Internal Structure." ),
        new_frame( monitors, computers, "CRT Screen." ),
        new_frame( keyboards, computers, "" ),
        new_frame( peripherals, computers, "There are many." ),
        new_frame( mouse, peripherals, "Not on all systems." ),
        new_frame( printers, peripherals, "Many Types." ),
        new_frame( plotters, peripherals,
            "Interface is important." ),
        new_frame( disc_controller, intern_strs, "Floppy." ),
        new_frame( extend_memory, intern_strs, "Extended." ),
        new_frame( mother_board, intern_strs, "Contains CPU." ),

        new_slot( computers, make_model, open, 0, 0, [],
            "IBM", "What is Make and Model." ),
```

```
new_slot( keyboards, function_keys, integer, 32, 0, [],
    "16", "Number of Function Keys." ),
new_slot( keyboards, connection, symbol, 0, 0, [direct,
    fiber_optic], "direct", "Keyboard interface." ),
new_slot( keyboards, number_pad, symbol, 0, 0, [yes, no],
    yes, "Is there one?" ),
new_slot( printers, no_columns, integer, 132, 0, [], "80",
    "Number of printer columns." ),
new_slot( printers, interface, symbol, 0, 0, ["RS-232",
    "IEEE-488", parallel], "RS-232",
    "Type of printer interface." ),
new_slot( printers, paper_feed, symbol, 0, 0,
    [tractor, carriage], tractor, "Which one?" ),
new_slot( printers, make_model, open, 0, 0, [],
    toshiba_1350, "What make and model?" ),
new_slot( extend_memory, amount_mem, integer, 640, 0, [],
    "64", "Amount of memory in K bytes." ),
new_slot( peripherals, printer_slot, frame, 0, 0, [],
    "", "Name of frame for this slot." ),

new_slot_value( keyboards, function_keys, "24" ),
new_slot_value( keyboards, connection, "direct" ),
new_slot_value( keyboards, number_pad, "no" ),
new_slot_value( peripherals, printer_slot, "printers" ),
new_slot_value( printers, interface, "parallel" ),
new_slot_value( printers, make_model, "Okidata" ).
```

Using the Frame System

To test this frame representation system, enter "load(computer)" as a goal. This statement loads all of the data from the "f_data.pro" file. By entering "list(values)," you will obtain the list of all of the slots and their values. The screen should look like this:

```
              SLOT VALUES
Frame            Slot             Value
computers        make_model       IBM
printers         no_columns       80
printers         paper_feed       tractor
extend_memory    amount_mem       64
keyboards        function_keys    24
keyboards        connection       direct
keyboards        number_pad       no
printers         interface        parallel
printers         make_model       Okidata
peripherals      printer_slot     printers

Press any key to continue.
```

If you want to obtain information on a particular slot, use the goal: "get_slot_value." Here is an example of what you will see when this goal is specified:

```
Goal: get_slot_value(printers,no_columns,X)
X=80
1 Solution
Goal:
```

Now that the basic structure is defined, new frames and slots can be added or slot values can be displayed or modified. The options for the "list" clause are:

```
values    - list all slot values
slots     - list all slots
frames    - list all frames
fcomments - list all frame comments
scomments - list all slot comments
```

To save the knowledge representation as it is stored in memory, use the "save" and "consult" predicates. Using "save(filename)" stores the asserted data in "filename." The "consult(filename)" reloads the asserted data. If you use the "load" clause as described in this example, you won't need these predicates. However, if you are entering a lot of information dynamically from Turbo Prolog, these may come in handy. Either way, the resulting file can be viewed with the Turbo Prolog editor. This approach provides a method for viewing the information that has been asserted during the course of running the frame system.

Adding Enhancements

A number of enhancements can be added to this frame representation. For example, a delete and modify frame can be written. However, to add these features a strategy must be developed to prevent a parent frame from being deleted until the child frames have been removed or relocated. Displaying the slots for a specific frame would also be of use as would the ability to copy or rename a slot or frame.

Another useful concept related to frame representation is called inheritance. Inheritance is best illustrated by an example. Looking at the computer knowledge representation previously discussed, you notice there is no "bus structure" slot on the extend memory frame. Instead of adding that slot, you could modify the "get_slot_value" clause to look for that slot at its parent frame. And if it didn't find it there, it could keep looking up the hierarchy of frames until the slot was found. This mechanism is commonly referred to as inheritance. This mechanism reduces the storage and setup requirements because general slots can be allocated at higher levels. This means that all slots at a given level receive the benefits of this information, thus eliminating the need for repeating the information.

There are two common types of inherited slots: member and explicit. Frames that inherit member slots only inherit the structure of the slot, such as defined by "new_slot." Explicit slots inherit the structure as well as the value of that slot. These slots can only have their structure modified at the frame where they are defined. Likewise, the explicit slot can only have its value modified at the defining frame.

There is also a special type of frame, known as a script, that is used to understand and represent scenes. Scripts, which consists of a set of slots, are used to describe a repeated or stereotyped sequence of events. For example, the sequence of events related to stopping at a service station for gas could be represented with a script. First you stop the car, tell the attendant what type and how much gas, the attendant washes the windows and checks the oil, you pay the attendant and drive off. Some of the major components or slots for a script consist of the entry conditions, results, props (or objects), roles (or people), tracks (or variations of a script), and scenes (or sequences of events).

Semantic Networks

The semantic network scheme for knowledge representation is more general than the frame representation presented in the previous section. With semantic networks, knowledge is represented by a set of nodes and arcs. In this scheme, a node symbolizes an object, a concept, or a situation, and an arc represents a relationship between two objects.

Semantic networks are usually structured as a directed graph. As an example, Figure 6.9 shows a semantic network for representing knowledge about airplanes. The circles represent the nodes and the lines connecting the nodes are the arcs. Note that there are different relationships represented by the arcs. The definitions of these relationships are:

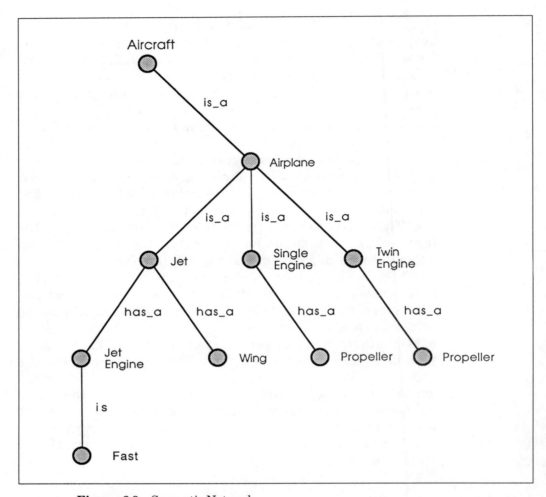

Figure 6.9   Semantic Network

Is-a   This relationship indicates that an object is a sub-
          class of another object. In the example, the seman-
          tic network shows that "airplane is an aircraft" and
          "jet is an airplane." In this respect the is-a relation-
          ship has a built-in hierarchy.

Has-a   The has-a relationship is used to indicate that an
          object consists of other parts or properties. In the
          example, the "jet has a jet engine" and the "single
          engine has a propeller."

Is   The is relationship is used to gove an object a value.
          In the example, the "jet engine is fast."

These relationships can easily be expressed in Turbo Prolog with simple predicates. For example the is-a relationship can be written as:

```
is_a(airplane, aircraft).
is_a(jet, airplane).
```

The has-a relationship can also be written in this form:

```
has_a(jet, wing).
has_a(single_engine, propeller).
```

Finally, the is relationship can be written:

```
is(jet_engine, fast).
```

In certain respects, semantic networks are similar to frames. The information or knowledge is encoded in the connections or arcs, thus allowing the representation of complex relationships. In this way, the knowledge representation is very efficient and quite effective. Semantic networks also support the concept of inheritance. Objects of lower classes can inherit the attributes of objects of higher classes.

Hints on Building a Knowledge Base

After exploring some of the different techniques for representing knowledge, such as representing knowledge with rules or logic, frames, scripts, and semantic networks, you might now have some questions about how to select the basic representation for a particular knowledge base. When choosing a knowledge representation, here are some of the important issues to consider:

- Will the expert or the user be responsible for the initial acquisition of the knowledge? How will the knowledge be initially acquired? Who will be responsible for modifying and maintaining it in the future? Will the knowledge base be dynamic?

- Will the structure of the knowledge be able to handle the necessary relationships in an efficient manner? Using a conventional address database as an example, there are a large number of fields of information for each entry. It would be very inefficient to use a representation with two field records: One field having the name and the second field the information of interest. By the time the address, city, state, zip, and phone were entered, the same name would be in the database five times.

- Will the structure of the representation allow the relevant knowledge to be separated from that which is not? This should be done without having to worry about the order in which the knowledge is added to the knowledge base, or its relative location in the knowledge base.

- How will this knowledge base be tested to ensure that the above constraints are met? How will you know if the knowledge base is inadequate or incorrect with missing rules or unforeseen interactions? What methods are available to ensure the knowledge remains reliable and does not become contradictory or redundant?

CHAPTER 7

Developing Expert Systems

Expert systems are among the most useful and interesting applications of artificial intelligence. Expert systems which model the expertise of a human expert are challenging to program. As you can imagine, it is difficult to capture the experience and knowledge of a human expert. To develop successful expert systems, it is necessary to adopt a different programming approach. The emphasis for developing expert systems should be placed on gathering, representing, and manipulating the knowledge of the expert. Fortunately, Turbo Prolog is an excellent language for developing expert systems. Because of both its declarative and procedural nature, and its built-in features for representing knowledge structures such as rules and facts, you can create expert systems in much less time than it would take if you were using a traditional procedural language such as C or Pascal.

In this final chapter the characteristics of experts and the concepts for developing expert systems are explored. The different types of expert systems are introduced and some real examples are presented. You will learn about the structure of expert systems and the fundamental concepts involved in designing them. In the second part of the chapter, the concepts of inference and reasoning techniques are combined with knowledge representation schemes to generate an expert system shell. To develop successful expert systems, it is important to have a good understanding of the whole cycle of development from problem selection to implementation, testing, and modification of an expert system solution.

What Makes an Expert an Expert?

The first step involved in learning how to develop expert systems is determining exactly what a human expert is and how human experts use their expertise. Frequently you meet people, such as doctors, accountants, and lawyers, who are experts or specialists in their field. These experts are usually specialists in a relatively narrow field or domain of expertise. They are successful at applying their knowledge and problem solving skills to solve specific problems. They do not, however, have the expertise to solve all problems. For example, you would not expect your accountant to provide you with expert advice about your stomach problem. The primary source of the expert's exceptional problem solving ability comes from the special knowledge, judgment, and experience that this person has compiled through years of training and work in the field.

In looking at experts, the first question that comes to mind is: What characteristics do experts have in common? First, experts solve problems that are often poorly defined or understood. And they do this with incomplete information and often without the resources, such as time, to perform a complete analysis. They handle this lack of structure by employing heuristics, or rules of thumb.

When confronted with a difficult problem, experts are able to restructure the pertinent information as well as their understanding of the problem. This allows them to divide the problem into smaller, more easily solved parts, or problems similar to ones already solved. Experts also know when to break the rules, determine the relevance of information, and obtain a solution without excessive resources. They solve problems using a minimal number of false starts and the least number of intermediate steps. Once a solution is obtained, they can explain the results and how their own reasoning process was used. In addition, experts can also find multiple solutions to a problem as well as recognize when a problem is outside their field of expertise.

Characteristics of an Expert System

From the above discussion, you can see that it is difficult to represent the characteristics of a human expert in a computer program. However, many successful programs have been created to perform like human experts. These expert systems, often referred to as knowledge based systems, are a class of computer program that can emulate the thought process of a human expert over a limited domain of expertise. Expert systems are often developed by human experts. The human expert attempts to represent methods and reasoning processes for solving specific problems using knowledge structures such as facts and rules.

Even if successful, expert systems can only provide a small extension to the expert's problem solving ability. The expert system has no real intelligence nor can it completely take the place of the human expert. As will be seen later, it is often used as a supplement to the expert. Many systems serve a role as an expert advisor. That is, they help experts solve problems by providing them with useful advice.

Many of the operations that a human expert performs when solving a problem, as discussed in the last section, are also found in an expert system. Expert systems ask questions, explain their reasoning process, and can acquire new knowledge. These and many of the other traits of an expert are represented in an expert system.

Types of Expert Systems

Just as there are many types of experts, there are also many types of expert systems. Before getting into the details of how expert systems are designed, it will help you to have some understanding of the different types of expert systems. The following sections provide some discussion about the important categories of expert systems shown in Figure 7.1.

Diagnosis

Diagnosis systems are used to perform tasks such as recommend remedies for illnesses, trouble-shoot electronics problems, debug problems in computer software and hardware, etc. Essentially, these systems look for problems and recommend solutions for the problems. Diagnosis expert systems are one of the most successful types of expert systems in use today. Such systems contain extensive knowledge bases which store the types of problems and related solutions for given diagnostic applications. Often this knowledge is stored in a heuristic structure such as a tree representation. For example, consider an expert system which diagnoses mechanical problems in an airplane. The major task of such a system is to determine which control component of the airplane is at fault. Figure 7.2 illustrates how the knowledge base for this expert system might be constructed. Note, the

Types of Expert Systems

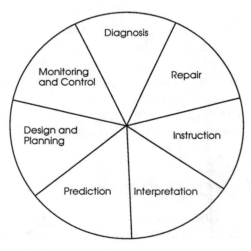

Figure 7.1   Categories of Expert Systems

hierarchy of the knowledge. In such a system, the program starts with the questions at the top of the tree and works its way down until the correct solution is found.

Many expert diagnosis systems are built with generic expert system shells and knowledge bases that are easily changeable. This means the same shell can be employed as the foundation for different applications. The developer only needs to provide different knowledge bases. The major drawbacks with diagnosis expert systems is that their knowledge base can grow exponentially for complex problems and they do not work well with intermittent data and incomplete knowledge.

Repair

Expert systems for repair applications are also very common. These systems are given a diagnosed problem for which they develop a repair plan. They then execute this plan to repair the problem. They have a knowledge structure similar to diagnosis systems but with the additional ability to schedule and control the decision. Repair expert systems have been successfully employed in many diverse fields including automotive repair, computer maintenance, communications networks, and avionics and space equipment repair.

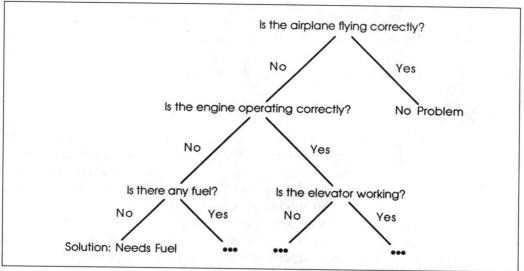

Figure 7.2   Knowledge Base for a Diagnostic Expert System

Instruction

Expert systems can be used to teach students. Instruction expert systems contain the knowledge and techniques for presenting instructional material. Often, these systems represent the subject matter as well as the students' learning performance. Such models provide the basis for decisions made by the expert system. Instruction expert systems use techniques found in diagnosis expert systems to diagnose weaknesses and recommend solutions for increasing a student's learning capacity. What's more, the fact that these systems are expert systems make them a powerful tool for learning because they can be asked to explain their decisions.

The use of instructional expert systems are on the increase. Many companies and educational environments are beginning to discover the benefits of using expert systems. The valuable knowledge of experts can be passed on to students in a cost-effective manner.

Interpretation

Interpretation systems analyze data to determine its significance and provide useful analysis. The knowledge base often contains models or scenarios as well as known relationships. Interpretation expert systems work well in applications where the data observed in a situation is reliable. In this respect, the problems with interpretation systems are incomplete, unreliable, and contradictory data. Examples of these systems include surveillance, image analysis, speech understanding, and signal interpretation.

Prediction

An important problem solving technique employed by many experts is prediction. Examples of this approach can be found in the techniques used by weather experts for determining future weather conditions. Prediction techniques can also be used in expert systems. These systems can infer or guess the consequences from observed situations. Many successful prediction expert systems have been written using probability as a technique to reduce the number of possible solutions to a problem. Prediction expert systems are used in weather forecasting, traffic and crop estimating, and military forecasting.

Design and Planning

Design and planning expert systems are used in applications ranging from mechanical engineering to business management. These systems aid designers and planners by providing them with the necessary expertise to help them make intelligent decisions. Such systems can help minimize constraints including cost, time, and availability of materials. They may employ a model to determine the effects of the planned activities. Design and planning expert systems can support activities such as computer system configuration, circuit layout, budgeting, building design, software development, counseling, and even magazine design.

Monitoring and Control

Expert systems can also be used in real time applications to monitor and control complex tasks. Monitoring and control expert systems are especially useful in applications where human experts cannot analyze information quick enough to respond to critical situations. The expert system can help the expert by comparing observed behavior with that represented in a computer model. Critical situations can be carefully monitored enabling tasks to be performed when they are not within specifications. The system can automatically perform or recommend actions to be performed based on a predicted course of events. These systems are currently used for applications including power plant and air traffic control, disease control, and numerous business applications.

Why Have Expert Systems?

Now that you understand what an expert system is and the types of expert systems that are in use, you might still be wondering why you should consider building an expert system to solve a programming problem. To answer this question, you might find it helpful to break it up into two parts:

1. What are the advantages of expert systems over conventional programming?
2. How do expert systems compare with human experts?

Expert Systems vs. Conventional Software

For many problems, expert systems have numerous advantages over conventional software. First, information or knowledge in the knowledge base is stored separately from the program control strategies. This simplifies modifications and updates to the knowledge base because the core of the expert system is not affected. In conventional software, the knowledge and the control flow are combined in the program code. If either changes, then the program code is modified and must be tested. Because of the separation between knowledge and control structures in an expert system, it is easier to develop prototypes and iteratively improve an expert system.

The second advantage expert systems have over conventional software is that expert systems represent data symbolically rather than numerically. A symbolic representation is closer to the way that humans represent knowledge, thus this approach is better suited for solving complex, expert-level problems. Heuristic or intelligent reasoning processes can also be used instead of the algorithmic processes used in conventional programs. This allows expert systems to work on problems where there are extremely large or combinatorial explosive solutions. For example, determining the next move in a chess game would require more time than the most patient chess player would wait if a conventional program tried to look at all possible moves.

Finally, expert systems also support uncertainty. Conventional software has no intrinsic mechanism for handling uncertainty. Unlike conventional software, expert systems often offer explanations as to why a question is asked or how decisions or conclusions are made.

How Expert Systems Compare with Human Experts

You have seen that the problem solving characteristics of an expert and an expert system are similar in some ways. On the other hand, the human expert has the ability to determine the level of his or her understanding, to know when to break the normal rules, and to restructure a problem to make it easier to solve. He or she also has a vast wealth of background knowledge or common sense. The primary advantage, however, is the most important characteristic, his or her intelligence. Also, human experts frequently use intuition to solve problems.

Nevertheless, expert systems have a number of advantages over the human expert. Besides being able to make decisions in fractions of the time it takes human experts, these systems are extremely thorough and tireless; even on the most mundane tasks, they can work 24 hours a day without breaks or vacation. Expert systems also raise the average performance of the human experts by incorporating the knowledge of more than one expert. Often, the very process of generating an expert system enables the expert to learn more about the field of expertise as well as increase understanding of his or her own thinking process. In addition, expert systems can teach new experts by providing expert opinions on how to solve various problems.

Unlike human experts, expert systems can be duplicated, allowing it to be cloned and placed on many systems and utilized by many users. With these systems, experts go where needed to many locations where human expertise is scarce. An expert system can capture the expertise of a valued expert, thus allowing a company to preserve it. This transfer of expertise allows the expert to retire, take a vacation, or go on to other tasks that could increase his or her level of expertise.

Components of an Expert System

Most expert systems are composed of an inference engine, a knowledge base, and some type of user interface. Figure 7.3 is an illustration of such an expert system. The inference engine, as presented in Chapter 4, is the main component of the expert system. It controls the reasoning process of the system. The knowledge base contains the necessary knowledge in the form of knowledge structures for the expert system. In many systems this knowledge is represented as rules and facts. Also, another component of the knowledge base is the

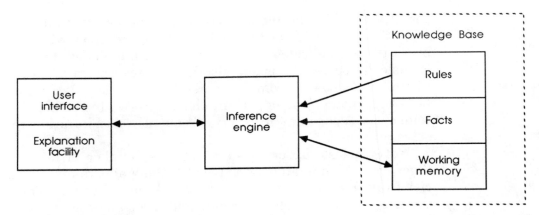

Figure 7.3   Components of an Expert System

working memory. The working memory contains the facts that are acquired by the expert system during its operation. These facts are not permanent, however. Finally, the user interface performs the task of communicating with the user. This component is responsible for receiving messages from the user and sending back messages to the user from the inference engine in the form of explanations.

One useful technique for building expert systems consists of creating a general inference engine and interface to the knowledge base. These systems are called expert shells or shells for short. In this chapter, a rule-based shell will be constructed in Turbo Prolog. The shell uses backward-chaining to process rules and facts stored in the knowledge base. Expert shells are useful tools for developing expert systems because they can be combined with different knowledge bases to generate systems for various applications. With the shell approach, you do not have to rewrite your program (inference engine) each time you develop a new application. As a programmer, your main task is one of collecting and representing the knowledge needed to solve a particular problem.

Building a Knowledge Base with Production Rules

Many techniques are used to represent knowledge such as logic, rules, frames, scripts, and semantic networks, as you discovered from reading Chapter 6. The expert shell developed here uses a form of rules called production rules. These rules are expressed in the standard IF-THEN format and they are used to represent relationships between facts. A rule for a medical diagnostic system might be constructed as:

```
IF
        patient's temperature is high
        AND
        patient's throat is irritated.


THEN
        patient has a cold
```

Production rules consist of two parts: antecedent(s), which function as conditions, and a conclusion. The statements "patient's temperature is high" and "patient's throat is irritated" are antecedents and the statement "patient has a cold" is the conclusion. Antecedents can be simple facts or they may refer to other rules. For example "patient's temperature is high" might define the rule:

```
IF
        patient's temperature is over 100F
THEN
        patient's temperature is high
```

A production rule representation has many advantages, some of which are:

```
Hierarchical Representation: rules can make refer-
ence to other rules, thus they have a built-in
hierarchy.

Natural Representation: rules are easy to write
because their structure is simple and is based on
a natural form.

Dynamic Representation: rules can be added to or
deleted from the system easily.
```

In the expert system developed in this section, the production rules are expressed in the following form:

```
RuleNumber: Conclusion
           IF
           Condition
```

The "RuleNumber" tag is used to identify the rule. Note also that the order of the conclusion and the condition is reversed. Production rules in this form are easily represented in Turbo Prolog. Also, with such a representation, the inference engine can easily search for a specified conclusion and, once found, the inference engine can try to verify the conclusion by proving the conditions.

The knowledge base for the expert system constructed in this chapter uses a user defined predicate—rule—to represent production rules. The form of this predicate is:

```
rule(rule_no, rule_head, rule_body).
```

The term, rule_no, refers to the number assigned to the rule. Rule_head is the head of the rule (conclusion) and rule_body is the body of the rule. The body defines the conditions which must be met in order for the conclusion to be valid. The rule body, represented as a list, is composed of other rules and/or facts. Here is an example:

```
rule(2,    isa(X,    man),    [    isa(X,human),
isa(X,male)]).
```

The conclusion, isa(X,man), represents the statement:

```
X is a man
```

and the condition part of this rule, [isa(X,human), isa(X,male)], represents:

```
IF
X is a human AND X is a male.
```

The condition part, which is represented as a list, can consist of other rules or facts. For example, the statement "isa(X,human)" might refer to another rule or might be a simple fact. For the body part of the rules used in the knowledge base constructed next, the condition list can be written in one of two forms:

```
(1)    [rule, fact, fact,...]
```

```
(2)    [fact, fact, fact,...]
```

where the term "rule" refers to those properties that are themselves names of rule heads and the term "facts" are conditions which must be verified by the inference engine. The first condition illustrates the case where the body of the rule is composed of another rule and a list of facts. The second form represents a body consisting of only facts.

A Sample Knowledge Base

Now that the representation scheme has been decided for the knowledge base, the next step is to build one. The first task in building the expert system consists of gathering the knowledge and representing it in the knowledge base. This is the most time intensive and difficult problem of building an expert system. To get the knowledge for an expert system, you must interview experts, read literature about the problem you are trying to solve, and collect only the knowledge which is appropriate to the problem domain. Here are the important steps that you should consider when building a knowledge base:

1. Identify the problem to be solved
2. Select the problem domain
3. Gather the knowledge
4. Select a knowledge representation
5. Represent the acquired knowledge
6. Test and refine the knowledge

The first step is the most important. You must be certain that the problem you are trying to solve is well defined before you begin acquiring and representing knowledge. Once you have a good understanding of the problem, the next step is to select the problem domain. This goal is accomplished by determining what the boundaries are for the problem you are trying to solve. In essence, you should be asking yourself the question: What knowledge must an expert have to solve this problem? To answer this, there are some additional questions to consider:

1. Which objects are involved?
2. What are the relationships between the objects?
3. What are the essential goals?

The last four steps outlined above represent the process of actually acquiring and building the knowledge base. Keep in mind, however, that this process is continuous. When constructing knowledge bases, you will discover that the knowledge has to be frequently modified. As you test out knowledge in your expert system, you will discover that some knowledge is inaccurate or incorrectly represented. This process of building knowledge bases is very similar to debugging a program.

To understand better what is involved in building a knowledge base, you should consider the following example. Assume you are planning a vacation and you need to decide which resort you want to stay at. One way to make this selection easier is to classify the resorts on the basis of their quality. Resorts can be classified by a rating system such as:

```
One-Star:    Poor quality resort
Two-Star:    Modest quality
Three-Star:  Good quality
Four-Star:   Excellent quality
```

The next step is to determine which characteristics or properties are needed to define the different categories. You could represent the properties by a set of production rules as shown:

```
Rule   1:   Resort has a bad location
               IF
                  Resort is on a busy street
Rule   2:   Resort has a good location
               IF
                  Resort is by the ocean
               OR
                  Resort is in the mountains
Rule   3:   Resort is unsatisfactory
               IF
                  (Resort has a bad location
               AND
                  Resort has poor service)
               OR
                  Resort has dirty rooms
Rule   4:   Resort is nice
               IF
                  Resort has a good location
```

```
                    AND
                        Resort has clean rooms
    Rule   5:   Resort is expensive
                    IF
                        Cost is over $100
    Rule   6:   Resort is inexpensive
                    IF
                        Cost is under $30
    Rule   7:   Resort is fancy
                    IF
                        Resort has a pool
                    AND
                        Resort has entertainment
                    AND
                        Resort has marble floors
    Rule   8:   Resort is a one star
                    IF
                        Resort is unsatisfactory
                    AND
                        Resort has bugs
                    AND
                        Resort needs repair
    Rule   9:   Resort is a two star
                    IF
                        (Resort is nice
                    AND
                        Resort has a pool
                    AND
                        Resort has good service)
                    OR
                        (Resort is inexpensive
                    AND
                        Resort has clean rooms)
    Rule 10:    Resort is a three star
                    IF
                        (Resort is a two star
                    AND
                        Resort has a good restaurant)
                    OR
                        (Resort has a good location
                    AND
                        Resort has entertainment)
    Rule 11:    Resort is a four star
                    IF
                        (Resort is fancy
```

```
          AND
              Resort has great service)
          OR
              (Resort is expensive
          AND
              Resort has a view
          AND
              Resort has good service)
```

Each of these production rules consist of a head, as in:

```
    Rule  8:    Resort is a one star
```

and a body:

```
        Resort is unsatisfactory
    AND
        Resort has bugs
    AND
        Resort needs repair
```

The head provides the rule number and the conclusion. The body represents the conditions that must be proved to verify the conclusion. Note that some rules make reference to other rules. Because of this structure, the rules have a built-in hierarchy. Rules 8, 9, 10, and 11 define the properties of the four different rating classifications and the other rules are used to

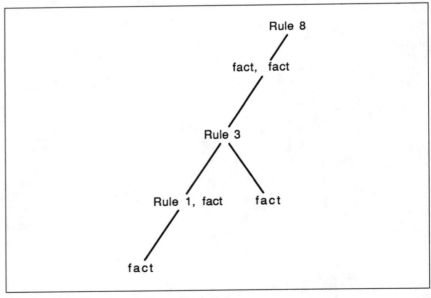

Figure 7.4   Representation of Rule 8

define additional properties. Figures 7.4, 7.5, 7.6, and 7.7 show the hierarchical structure for each of the main rules. The AND and OR operators are used to join conditions. For example, in Figure 7.4, the tree representation shows that rule 8 consists of sub-rules rule 3 and rule 1. To verify rule 8 is valid, two conditions must be met: rule 3 must be true and the two facts, "Resort has bugs" and "Resort needs repair" must be proven. To prove these facts (conditions), the inference engine must query the user when these conditions are encountered. Rule 3, on the other hand, can be verified if rule 1 and the fact "Resort has poor service" is proven, or the fact "Resort has dirty rooms" is proven.

Now that these rules are defined, the next step is to represent them in Turbo Prolog. First, you must select an appropriate domain to represent the parts of each rule. On the following page are the domain definitions used in the example knowledge base.

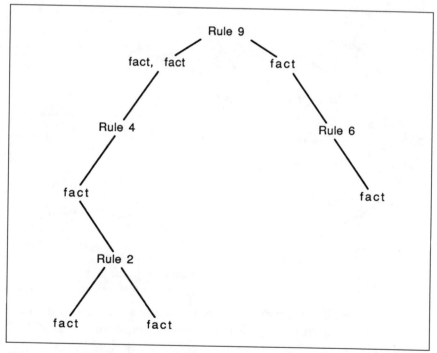

Figure 7.5   Representation of Rule 9

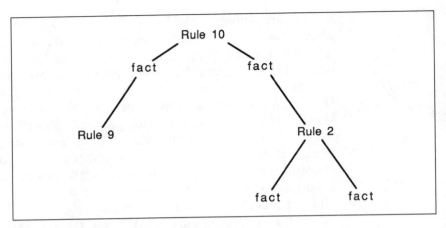

Figure 7.6   Representation of Rule 10

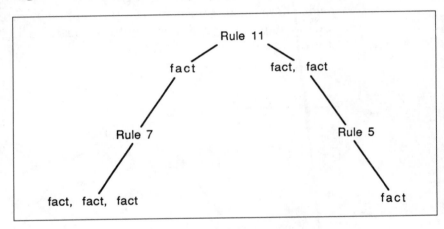

Figure 7.7   Representation of Rule 11

```
domains
  data_list = data_type*
  data_type = is(symbol,symbol);
              has(symbol,symbol);
              is_on(symbol,symbol);
              is_in(symbol,symbol);
              is_by(symbol,symbol);
              cost(symbol, symbol);
              needs(symbol, symbol)
```

Each term represents either a rule head or a condition part of
a rule body. For example, the term:

```
is(symbol, symbol)
```

is used to represent rule 4, "Resort is nice," with the expression:

```
is(X, nice)
```

On the other hand, the term:

```
cost(symbol, symbol)
```

is used to represent a fact such as:

```
cost(X, over_100)
```

As stated earlier, rules are represented with a Prolog predicate. This predicate is defined as:

```
rule(integer, data_type, data_list)
```

With this representation, a complete rule is written as:

```
rule(4, is(X, nice), [ has(X, good_location),
                       has(X, clean_rooms)] ).
```

which expresses:

```
Rule 4:    Resort is nice
       IF
           Resort has a good location
       AND
           Resort has clean rooms
```

Note the term, "has(X, good_location)," refers to rule 2, thus illustrating the principle that rules can "call" other rules.

The knowledge base also contains a series of questions which relate to the facts represented in the knowledge base. A question is of the form:

```
question(question_no, fact).
```

The first argument represents the question number and the second argument is the fact for which the question applies. As an example, one of the questions in the knowledge base is shown here:

```
question(1, is_on(X,busy_street)):-
      write("Is ", X, " on a busy street?").
```

This question refers to the fact "is_on(X,busy_street)." Whenever this fact is processed with a call, such as:

```
question(1, is_on(hilton, busy_street).
```

you will be asked the question:

```
Is hilton on a busy street?
```

The inference engine selects a question whenever an unknown fact is encountered. Because of this, it is necessary to include a question for every fact in the knowledge base.

Type in the knowledge base and give it the name "resort.kwl." The following shows the complete listing.

Listing 7.1

```
/*        Resort Knowledge Base       */

domains
        data_list = data_type*
        data_type = is(symbol,symbol);
                    has(symbol,symbol);
                    is_on(symbol,symbol);
                    is_in(symbol,symbol);
                    is_by(symbol,symbol);
                    cost(symbol, symbol);
                    needs(symbol, symbol)

predicates
        rule(integer, data_type, data_list)
        question(integer, data_type)

clauses
        rule(1, has(X, bad_location), [ is_on(X, busy_street)] ).

        rule(2, has(X, good_location), [ is_by(X, ocean) ] ).

        rule(2, has(X, good_location), [ is_in(X, mountains) ] ).

        rule(3, is(X, unsatisfactory), [ has(X, bad_location),
                                         has(X,poor_service)] ).

        rule(3, is(X, unsatisfactory), [ has(X,dirty_rooms)] ).

        rule(4, is(X, nice), [ has(X, good_location),
                               has(X, clean_rooms)] ).

        rule(5, is(X, expensive), [ cost(X,over_100) ] ).

        rule(6, is(X, inexpensive), [ cost(X,under_30) ] ).
```

```
rule(7, is(X, fancy), [has(X,pool), has(X, entertainment),
                    has(X, marble_floors)] ).

rule(8, is(X, one_star), [is(X, unsatisfactory), has(X, bugs),
                    needs(X,repair)] ).

rule(9, is(X, two_star), [is(X, nice), has(X, pool),
                    has(X,good_service)] ).

rule(9, is(X, two_star), [is(X, inexpensive), has(X, clean_rooms) ]).

rule(10, is(X, three_star), [is(X, two_star),
                    has(X, good_restaurant) ]).

rule(10, is(X, three_star), [has(X, good_location),
                    has(X, entertainment) ] ).

rule(11, is(X, four_star), [is(X, fancy), has(X, great_service) ]).

rule(11, is(X, four_star), [is(X, expensive), has(X, view),
                    has(X,good_service)] ).

question(1, is_on(X,busy_street)):-
      write("Is ", X, " on a busy street?").

question(2, is_by(X,ocean)):-
      write("Is ", X, " by the ocean?").

question(3, is_in(X,mountains)):-
      write("Is ", X, " in the mountains?").

question(4, has(X, poor_service)):-
      write("Does ", X, " have poor service?").

question(5, has(X, good_service)):-
      write("Does ", X, " have good service?").

question(6, has(X, clean_rooms)):-
      write("Does ", X, " have clean rooms?").

question(7, has(X, pool)):-
      write("Does ", X, " have a pool?").

question(8, has(X, dirty_rooms)):-
      write("Does ", X, " have dirty rooms?").

question(9, cost(X, over_100)):-
      write("Does ", X, " cost over $100?").

question(10, cost(X, under_30)):-
      write("Does ", X, " cost under $30?").
```

(continued)

```
question(11, has(X, entertainment)):-
      write("Does ", X, " have entertainment?").

question(12, has(X, marble_floors)):-
      write("Does ", X, " have marble floors?").

question(13, has(X, bugs)):-
      write("Does ", X, " have bugs?").

question(14, needs(X, repair)):-
      write("Does ", X, " need repair?").

question(15, has(X, great_service)):-
      write("Does ", X, " have great service?").

question(16, has(X, view)):-
      write("Does ", X, " have a view?").

question(17, has(X, good_restaurant)):-
      write("Does ", X, " have a good restaurant?").
```

If you look closely at the knowledge base you will notice that some of the rules are represented with more than one predicate. As an example, rule 3 is written:

```
rule(3, is(X, unsatisfactory),    [ has(X, bad_location),
                                      has(X,poor_service)]).
rule(3, is(X, unsatisfactory),    [ has(X,dirty_rooms)] ).
```

which is a representation of the original rule:

```
Rule 3:    Resort is unsatisfactory
      IF
          (Resort has a bad location
      AND
          Resort has poor service)
      OR
          Resort has dirty rooms
```

To represent the OR connective, multiple clauses are used. When the inference engine selects rules from the knowledge base, it selects the first rule that matches a specified rule head. If the selected rule fails, the inference engine looks for other matching rules. In essence, the multiple clauses indicate that the OR connective is used.

Building the Shell

Now that the knowledge base is constructed, the next step is to write the expert shell. Keep in mind, however, that the shell constructed in this section can be used for different knowledge bases. The only requirement is that the knowledge base must be represented in the form presented in the previous section.

The main predicate in the shell is "process." This predicate accepts a query as shown:

```
process(Query):-
       inference(Query),
       write("Your question ", Query, " has been
       proved.").
process(Query):-
       write("Your question ", Query, " cannot be
       proved.")
```

The query should be in the form of a question or rule. For example, if you wanted to ask the expert system if a specified resort has a certain rating, you would use the goal:

```
process(is(hilton, two_star)).
```

thus, asking the system:

```
Is the Hilton a two-star resort?
```

The expert system would use its inference mechanism to determine the answer to this query. Here is a possible dialogue that you might have with the expert system if you specify such a goal. Note that the responses "yes" and "no" are supplied by you:

```
Is hilton by the ocean? no
Is hilton in the mountains? yes
Does hilton have clean rooms? yes
Does hilton have a pool? yes
Does hilton have good service? yes
Your question is(hilton,two_star) has been proved.
```

The predicate process calls inference which serves as the heart of this shell. Inference is implemented as a recursive predicate:

```
inference(Query):-
        not(rule(_, Query, _)).
inference(Query):-
        check_rule(No, Query, Cond_list),
        get_first(Cond_list, Cond),
        inference(Cond),
        process_rule(No, Cond, Cond_list), !.
```

Inference takes a rule and searches through the knowledge base until a fact in a rule body is encountered. As an example, Figure 7.8 shows the control flow of inference with the query, "is(hilton, two_star)."

The first inference predicate stops the recursion when a fact is encountered. A fact is any term that does not have a rule head. For example, the term "has(X, dirty_rooms)" is a fact because there are no matching rule heads in the knowledge base.

The second inference predicate calls itself until the first predicate succeeds. Once the recursion stops, inference calls process_rule which is shown here with rmv_rule:

```
process_rule(No, Query, Cond_list):-
                rmv_rule(Query, Cond_list, Nl), !,
                process_facts(No, Nl).
rmv_rule(Query, Cond_list, Nl):-
                rule(_, Query,_),
                delete(Query, Cond_list, Nl).
rmv_rule(_, Cond_list, Cond_list).  /* only facts */
```

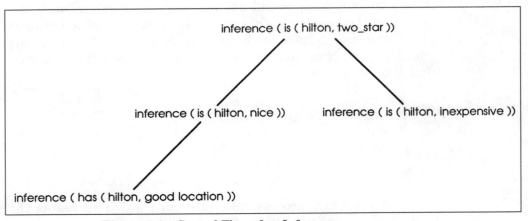

Figure 7.8 Control Flow of an Inference

These predicates process a rule list of the form:

```
[rule, fact, fact ...]
        or
[fact, fact, fact ...]
```

by removing the rule from the list if it is present. Note, that the list tool delete, which was developed in Chapter 3 is used here to remove the rule from the list. Once the list is adjusted, the predicate process_facts is called. This predicate processes a fact by asking a question:

```
process_facts(_, []).   /* no more facts left */


process_facts(Rno, Cond_list):-
        get_first(Cond_list, Prop),
        question(_, Prop),
        getresponse(Response), !,
        validresponse(Response, y),
        delete(Prop, Cond_list, New_list),
        process_facts(Rno, New_list).
```

The first predicate looks for the condition where the list of facts is empty. When this condition occurs, the predicate succeeds. The second process_facts asks you to verify if the given fact is correct or not. For example, if process_facts is called with the following:

```
process_facts(2 [is_by(hilton, ocean)]).
```

the predicate will respond with:

```
Is hilton by the ocean?
```

If you answer no to this question, this predicate fails and causes the inference engine to backtrack and search for another rule. On the other hand, if you answer yes, the predicate succeeds and the inference engine will move on to process the next rule.

The complete shell is included next. The include file is the knowledge base constructed in the previous section. You should type in the following program and try out some examples.

Listing 7.2

```
/* Expert System Shell */

include "resort.kwl"

predicates
        inference(data_type)
         check_rule(integer, data_type, data_list)
         process_rule(integer, data_type, data_list)
        process_facts(integer, data_list)
        getresponse(symbol)
        validresponse(symbol, symbol)
        get_first(data_list, data_type)
         delete(data_type, data_list, data_list)
        process(data_type)
        rmv_rule(data_type, data_list, data_list)
        check_ans(symbol, symbol)

clauses
        process(Query) :-
                inference(Query),
                write("Your question ", Query, " has been proved.").

        process(Query) :-
                write("Your question ", Query, " cannot be proved.").

        inference(Query) :-
                not(rule(_, Query, _)).

        inference(Query) :-
                check_rule(No, Query, Cond_list),
                get_first(Cond_list, Cond),
                inference(Cond),
                process_rule(No, Cond, Cond_list), !.

        check_rule(No, Query, Cond_list):- !,
                rule(No, Query, Cond_list).

        process_rule(No, Query, Cond_list):-
                rmv_rule(Query, Cond_list, Nl), !,
                process_facts(No, Nl).

        rmv_rule(Query, Cond_list, Nl):-
                rule(_, Query,_),
                delete(Query, Cond_list, Nl).

        rmv_rule(_, Cond_list, Cond_list).        /* only facts */

        process_facts(_, []).      /* no more facts left */
```

```
process_facts(Rno, Cond_list):-
      get_first(Cond_list, Prop),
      question(_, Prop),
      getresponse(Response), !,
      validresponse(Response, y),
      delete(Prop, Cond_list, New_list),
      process_facts(Rno, New_list).

getresponse(R):-
      readln(Ask),
      check_ans(Ask, Rep), !,
      R=Rep;
      nl, write("Try another answer please"),nl,
      getresponse(R).

check_ans(yes, y).
check_ans(y, y).
check_ans(n, n).
check_ans(no, n).

validresponse(R,y):-
      R=y.

get_first([H|_], H).

delete(_,[ ], []).

delete(Head, [Head|Tail], Tail):-!.

delete(Token, [Head|Tail], [Head|Result]) :- !,
      delete(Token, Tail, Result).
```

After the program is loaded and compiled, you can test out questions by using the goal, process. As you run different examples, you will notice that some of the rules in the knowledge base depend on other rules. For example, rule 8 calls rule 3 which in turn calls rule 1. It is helpful to keep in mind the hierarchical representation of these rules shown in Figures 7.4, 7.5, 7.6, and 7.7 when running the shell. Of course, because the shell is generic, you can create other knowledge bases and test out the reasoning capability of this shell.

Summary of the Shell

The shell built in the previous section is very powerful because it can work with different knowledge bases. In this respect, the shell performs the function of a rule interpreter as shown in Figure 7.9. Rules are read from the knowledge base

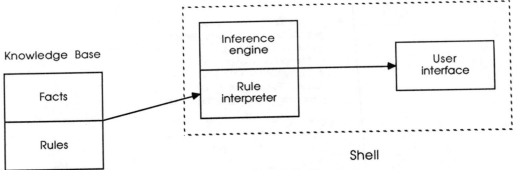

Figure 7.9   Function of an Expert Shell

and interpreted according to the user's response. If a selected rule fails, the inference engine attempts to find another rule to solve a specified question or goal.

Unfortunately, the expert system does not have the capability to show you its reasoning. If you ask the system a question, it will try and solve your query by asking you questions which are derived from the rules stored in its knowledge base. When the expert system asks you a question, you do not know why it is asking you such a question. The expert system can, however, be modified to support this feature as you will see in the following section.

Improving the Shell

Two additional features can easily be added to the shell to improve its performance. The first feature will allow you to dynamically add facts to the knowledge base and the second feature provides you with the capability of asking the system for explanations. The first feature is implemented with the add_fact predicate as shown:

```
add_fact(Fact):-
        not(storedfacts(Fact)),
        assert(storedfacts(Fact)).

add_fact(Fact):-
        nl,
        write(Fact, " is already stored in knowledge
        base"), nl.
```

Add_fact asserts a fact to the working memory part of the knowledge base which is represented with the database predicate:

```
database
     storedfacts(data_type)
```

This declaration must be added to the knowledge base file. Note that add_fact also tests to see if the fact is already in the knowledge base. If you try to add a fact that is already present, this predicate prints out a message to warn you.

Because the system now has a working memory, it can prove a fact by first testing to see if the fact has already been represented in the working memory. The predicate, check_fact, must be added to test for existing facts. Here is the new predicate:

```
check_fact(_, Fact):-
        storedfacts(Fact),
        write("\nUsing fact — ", Fact), nl.

check_fact(Rlst, Fact):-
        question(_, Fact),
        getresponse(Response),
        validresponse(Response, Fact, Rlst).
```

Check_fact tests to see if the fact being processed is presently in the working memory. If such a fact is found, the expert system uses this fact and therefore does not need to ask you to validate the fact.

The second feature, the explanation facility, is also easy to add to the shell. In order to implement this feature, the main inference predicate must be modified. Note the change:

```
inference(Query,_):-
   not(rule(_, Query, _)).

inference(Query, Rlst):-
        rule(No, Query, Cond_list),
        addl(No, Rlst, Nrlst),
        get_first(Cond_list, Cond),
        inference(Cond, Nrlst),
        process_rule(Nrlst, Cond, Cond_list), !.
```

Inference now contains a second argument. This argument is used to hold the list of rule numbers which refer to the rules that the system has examined. Once the inference engine accesses the knowledge base, it keeps a list of the rules that it has matched.

For example, if you provide a query such as:

```
is(kings_inn, two_star)
```

the inference engine will match rules 9, 4, and 2 and these numbers will be added to the rule list with the predicate addl. When the first inference predicate succeeds and thus stops the recursion, the rule list will contain:

```
Rlst = [2,4,9]
```

The predicate responsible for providing you with explanations is process_why as shown:

```
process_why([]).

process_why([Head|Tail]):- !,
        process_why(Tail),
        display_rule(Head).

display_rule(H):-
        rule(H, Rprop, _),
        write("\nProcessing rule ", H, ": ", Rprop), nl.
```

Process_why contains two parts. The first predicate tests for the case where the rule list is empty and the second predicate uses recursion to step through the list. The rules are processed in the reverse order, thus this predicate functions like the reverse tool developed in Chapter 3. Display_rule is responsible for writing the explanation to the screen.

When you now specify a query for the expert system and you are asked to verify a fact, you have the option of asking the system to tell you why it is asking you to verify that fact. For example, if you provide the query:

```
is(hilton, three_star)
```

the inference engine examines the rules in the knowledge base and then asks the question:

```
Is hilton by the ocean?
```

If you respond with "w" or "why," the system will tell you why you are being asked this question. In this case, the response is:

```
Processing rule 10: is(_,three_star)
Processing rule 9: is(_,two_star)
Processing rule 4: is(_,nice)
Processing rule 2: has(_,good_location)
```

Here the inference engine informs you that this question is being asked to solve rule 2 which is needed to solve rule 4 which is needed to solve rule 9, etc. In essence, this simple explanation shows you the dependency level of the rules.

Adding a New Front-End

The final change to this program is the new front-end represented with the start_exp predicate. This predicate displays a window and provides you with a small menu of options. From this menu you can add facts to the knowledge base (working memory), initialize the working memory, or specify a query for the expert system.

When you now specify facts or queries with the new system, they must be converted from character strings to a user-defined domain type (term). Turbo Prolog provides a built-in predicate for reading terms, readterm. Unfortunately, this predicate only reads terms from a file. To solve this problem, a new predicate has been added to the shell:

```
convert(Sym,Term):-
    openwrite(dest, "convt.dat"),
    writedevice(dest),
    write(Sym),
    closefile(dest),
    openread(dest, "convt.dat"),
    readdevice(dest),
    readterm(data_type, Term),
    closefile(dest),
    readdevice(keyboard).
```

Convert writes your fact or query to a file and then reads back the query or fact as a term. The only new requirement for running this program is that you must include quotes (" ") around the terms of a query or fact. For example, when you are asked:

```
What is your query?
```

you must enter a response of the form:

```
is("hilton","two_star")
```

The new shell is listed here. You should type in the following program now and test out its new features.

Listing 7.3

```
/* Expert System Shell Version 2 */

domains
        intl = integer*
        file = dest

include "resort.kwl"          /* Knowledge Base */

predicates
        proc_user(char)
        start_exp()
        inference(data_type, intl)
        process_rule(intl, data_type, data_list)
        process_facts(intl, data_list)
        getresponse(symbol)
        validresponse(symbol, data_type, intl)
        get_first(data_list, data_type)
        delete(data_type, data_list, data_list)
        process(data_type)
        rmv_rule(data_type, data_list, data_list)
        check_ans(symbol, symbol)
        add_fact(data_type)
        check_fact(intl, data_type)
        process_why(intl)
        display_rule(integer)
        clear_facts
        addl(integer, intl, intl)
        repeat
        convert(symbol, data_type)

clauses
        start_exp :-
        makewindow( 1, 7, 7, "Expert System", 1, 1, 20, 70 ),
        repeat(),
        write( " \n\n* * * * * * * * * * * * * * * *\nOptions" ),
        write( "\ni - initialize, a - add fact" ),
        write( "\nq - Quit, r - Run" ),
        write( "\nEnter option (i/a/q/r) :  " ),
        readchar( Choice ),
        proc_user( Choice ).

proc_user( 'q' ).

proc_user( 'r' ) :-
        write( "\nWhat is your query?  " ),
        readln(Query),
        convert(Query, Term),
        process(Term), !,
        fail.
```

```
proc_user( 'i' ) :-
     write( "\nReset - Clear out all Information (y/n)." ),
     readln( Response ),
     Response = y,
     clear_facts,
     fail.

proc_user( 'a' ) :-
     write("\nEnter fact to add to the knowledge base: " ),
     readln(Resp),
     convert(Resp, Fact),
     add_fact(Fact), !,
     fail.

convert(Sym,Term) :-
     openwrite(dest, "convt.dat"),
     writedevice(dest),
     write(Sym),
     closefile(dest),
     openread(dest, "convt.dat"),
     readdevice(dest),
     readterm(data_type, Term),
     closefile(dest),
       readdevice(keyboard).

process(Query) :-
     inference(Query,_),
     write("Your question ", Query, " has been proved.").

process(Query) :-
     write("Your question ", Query, " cannot be proved.").

inference(Query,_) :-
     not(rule(_, Query, _)).

inference(Query, Rlst) :-
     rule(No, Query, Cond_list),
     addl(No, Rlst, Nrlst),
     get_first(Cond_list, Cond),
     inference(Cond, Nrlst),
     process_rule(Nrlst, Cond, Cond_list), !.

process_rule(Rlst, Query, Cond_list) :-
     rmv_rule(Query, Cond_list, Nl), !,
     process_facts(Rlst, Nl).

rmv_rule(Query, Cond_list, Nl) :-
     rule(_, Query,_),
     delete(Query, Cond_list, Nl).

rmv_rule(_, Cond_list, Cond_list).          /* only facts */
```

(continued)

```
process_facts(_, []).        /* no more facts left */

process_facts(Rlst, Cond_list):-
        get_first(Cond_list, Prop),
        check_fact(Rlst, Prop), !,
        delete(Prop, Cond_list, New_list),
        process_facts(Rlst, New_list).

getresponse(R):-
        readln(Ask),
        check_ans(Ask, Rep), !,
        R=Rep;
        write("\nTry another answer please\n"),
        getresponse(R).

check_ans(yes, y).
check_ans(y, y).
check_ans(n, n).
check_ans(no, n).
check_ans(why, w).
check_ans(w, w).

add_fact(Fact):-
        not(storedfacts(Fact)),
        assert(storedfacts(Fact)).

add_fact(Fact):-
        nl,
        write(Fact, " is already stored in knowledge base"), nl.

check_fact(_, Fact):-
        storedfacts(Fact),
        write("\nUsing fact  — ", Fact), nl.

check_fact(Rlst, Fact):-
        question(_, Fact),
        getresponse(Response),
        validresponse(Response, Fact, Rlst).

validresponse(y, _,_).

validresponse(w, Fact, Rlst):-
        process_why(Rlst), !,
        check_fact(Rlst, Fact).

process_why([]).

process_why([Head|Tail]):- !,
        process_why(Tail),
        display_rule(Head).

display_rule(H):-
        rule(H, Rprop, _),
        write("\nProcessing rule ", H, ": ", Rprop), nl.
```

```
clear_facts :-
      retract(storedfacts(_)), fail.

clear_facts.

addl(Mem, L, [Mem | L]).

get_first([H|_], H).

delete(_,[ ], []).

delete(Head, [Head|Tail], Tail):-!.

delete(Token, [Head|Tail], [Head|Result]) :- !,
      delete(Token, Tail, Result).

repeat.

repeat :- repeat.
```

Working with Shells

The shell developed in this chapter uses a simple technique of sequentially searching a knowledge base of production rules. The rules are examined in the order in which they are represented; thus, the structure and order of the knowledge base determines the performance of the expert system. The production rule knowledge base is easy to create for small expert systems. Of course if you are planning to create a large-scale expert system, you should investigate other alternatives of representing knowledge such as frames or semantic networks.

Commercial expert system shells offer other features that were not incorporated in the simple Turbo Prolog shell. These features include more sophisticated user interfaces, extensive explanation facilities, and uncertainty factors. You could, however, add these features to the shell developed in this chapter to create a more useful expert system development tool. For example, a trace predicate could be included to keep track of the reasoning process of the inference engine. After the expert system solves a goal, you could ask it to explain how it determined its solution.

Who Is Benefiting from Expert Systems?

As a final note, you might find it interesting to consider some of the professions that are currently benefiting from the use of expert systems. Expert system technology is having a major impact on the way many programmers and software developers approach the art of problem solving. This section provides some discussion about the current applications of expert systems.

Engineering and Science

As the fields of engineering and science become more technical and specialized, it becomes more and more difficult to keep up with the changes in technology. Because of the specialized nature of technology, most scientific and engineering projects require experts in many disciplines. Unfortunately, due to the shortage of experts, this expertise is not always available when needed. Expert systems are rapidly providing a solution to this problem. The following examples will illustrate some technical uses of expert systems.

Weld selector is an expert system that advises welding engineers on how to select materials for the welding process. This selection is complicated by such factors as the chemical and physical composition of the metals being welded, possible atmospheric contamination, size and position of the weld, and the welding technique employed. If you consider the large number of products and structures that are composed of welded parts, this expert system provides a very useful function. Weldselector was developed by the Colorado School of Mine (CSM) and the American Welding Institute (AWI).

SpinPro, developed by Beckman Instruments, is an expert system that helps scientists choose from a large number of options for their ultracentrifuge. The ultracentrifuge can reach 100,000 revolutions a minute with forces over 60,000 times the force of gravity. Speed, suspension fluid, container size, and length of run are only a few of the variables that must be determined. If a researcher doesn't make an efficient choice of options, the run time can be unnecessarily long and the separation of material very ineffective. SpinPro, a PC based expert system, contains the expertise of a leading expert in ultracentrifuge techniques. It can be placed with every ultracentrifuge user, providing expert advise.

Business and Management

Although trailing the technical community, a number of expert systems are now commercially available for business applications. Because the business community is experiencing a tremendous increase in the amount of information processed daily, in the complexity of decisions made, and in the growing level of specialization, expert systems are a needed tool.

Top level management uses expert systems to monitor their organization. The expert system analyzes the information generated day to day, such as accounting and operations costs. It can detect major problems and watch for business trends. Expert system technology can also model the consequences of major corporate decisions such as organizational restructuring, buy-outs, and mergers.

The Home Computer User

Finally, expert systems are now finding their way into our home computers. One successful system, Line Expert has been developed to solve computer communication problems. This expert system, developed in Turbo Prolog, provides you with the diagnostic expertise to help you configure modems, serial cards, cabling, and communications software. Line Expert works in the same way as a real data communications expert. It has knowledge about different hardware and software products and the types of symptoms that occur when a computer user has communication problems.

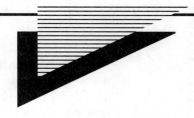

Glossary

Active Knowledge   *See Dynamic Knowledge.*

Algorithm   A procedure that specifies a logical step-wise strategy for solving a specific problem.

Argument   The parameters of a clause or functor. Arguments consist of both constant terms and variables.

Artificial Intelligence (AI)   A branch of computer science dedicated to the development of computer "intelligence."

Artificial Language   The languages, such as programming languages, used by people to communicate with computers.

Attribute   The definable properties of an object. For example, the property intelligence is an attribute of the object person.

Augmented Transition Network (ATN)   An extended recursive transition network that has the capability to recognize and recreate natural language sentences.

Backtracking   The control strategy built into Turbo Prolog which allows a program to search backward to find alternative solutions to a problem.

Backward-Chaining   The process of starting with a goal state and working backward with an assumption in order to prove the specified goal. Backward-chaining is the reasoning process often used in expert systems. *See also Forward-Chaining.*

Binding   The process of assigning a value to a variable.

Bound Variable   A variable that has been assigned a specified value. In Turbo Prolog, variables stay bound for the duration of a clause.

Certainty Factor   A value used to measure the confidence of a relationship or fact. Certainty factors are often used in expert systems. A typical certainty factor ranges from -1 to 1, where -1 represents a condition of the greatest uncertainty and 1 represents a condition of the greatest certainty.

Clause   A fact or rule. Clauses are defined in Turbo Prolog with the clause statement.

Complex Objects   Objects that can have multiple definitions and attributes.

Compound Goal   A goal consisting of more than one sub-goal.

Confidence Factor   *See Certainty Factor.*

Cut (!)   A Turbo Prolog operator that is used to stop backtracking in a program.

Decision Tree   A tree representation for the decisions and sub-decisions needed to solve a given problem.

Declarative Knowledge   Knowledge which can be represented as data in the form of facts or rules.

Declarative Language   A language such as Turbo Prolog that allows programmers to solve problems by specifying the constraints in the form of facts and rules.

Deep Knowledge   Knowledge that is based on the theories, facts, and principles of a specific topic. *See also Surface Knowledge.*

Deterministic Program   A program or algorithm that is capable of finding only one solution to a specific problem.

Diagnostic System   An expert system that solves diagnostic problems. Expert systems in this category include automotive diagnostic, general mechanical diagnostic, etc.

Domain   The definable boundaries of knowledge relating to a given topic.

Dynamic Database   A database that changes during the course of a program. Dynamic databases are implemented in Turbo Prolog with the database predicate.

Dynamic Knowledge   Knowledge that is acquired over time.

Expert System   Computer programs that contain the knowledge and expertise of human experts. Expert systems are one of the most popular and successful applications of artificial intelligence.

Expert System Shell   A tool that is used to build expert systems. The expert system shell consists of an inference engine, knowledge interface, and user interfaces.

Fact   A statement or premise about one or more objects that is true. Facts are easily written in Turbo Prolog with user-defined clauses.

Fail   A standard Turbo Prolog operator that forces backtracking to occur in a program.

Formal Reasoning   The process of using simple logic to make conclusions about objects.

Forward-Chaining   The process of starting with an assumption and working forward to find a valid goal. *See also Backward-Chaining.*

Frame Representation   A technique of knowledge representation. *See also Frames.*

Frames   A type of knowledge structure useful for representing complex relationships about objects. Frames function like tables or questionnaires and use locations called slots to store attributes.

Free Variable   A variable that has not been assigned a value.

Functor   A term used to describe a complex object in Turbo Prolog.

Goal   A problem to be solved in a Turbo Prolog program.

Goal State   A condition that must be met in order to solve a specified goal. A goal state typically represents the known facts, relationships, and attributes that are related to the final goal.

Goal Tree   A tree structure is used to represent the organization of a goal. The goal tree indicates the necessary sub-goals that must be met in order to prove a goal.

Heuristic   A technique or structure used in programs to improve the performance of searching for solutions. One common heuristic structure is represented by a tree.

Heuristic Knowledge   Knowledge that has a built-in hierarchical or top-down order.

Hierarchy   A network structure in which some objects are subordinate to other objects. A common tree structure is often used to represent object hierarchy.

Inference   The process of deriving new facts from old facts and rules.

Inference Engine   The reasoning mechanism of an expert system. Inference engines make deductions based on known facts and user responses.

Inheritance   The process of deriving values and relationships for objects based on the attributes and values of other objects. Inheritance is often used in frame-based representation systems.

Knowledge   A collection of rules, facts, properties, heuristics, and relationships needed to solve a specific problem.

Knowledge Acquisition   The science and art of gathering the necessary knowledge to solve a specific problem.

Knowledge Base   A collection of all the knowledge in the form of rules, facts, relationships, and attributes needed for an expert system.

Knowledge Engineer   An individual who gathers and represents knowledge for expert system applications. Knowledge engineers work closely with human experts.

Knowledge Structure   Structures that are used to represent objects, facts, rules, relationships, procedures, and attributes. Knowledge structures are developed with traditional data structures and other structures such as frames, semantic networks, and scripts.

List   An ordered collection of objects and attributes.

Meta-rule   A rule that defines other rules.

Modus Ponens   The fundamental inference rule used in formal logic systems. The *modus ponens* rule states the following principle: If (A is true) and (A and B are true) then B is true.

Natural Language   The language people use to communicate with each other.

Non-Deterministic Program   A program that is capable of finding multiple solutions to a specified problem.

Object   A conceptual or physical entity that can be expressed with attributes and relationships.

Parsing   The process of examining an expression by dividing it up into components such as symbols, words, and other structures.

Planning Systems Expert systems that are used to help people plan out complex tasks.

Predicate A function that can only have a true or false value. Predicates are used to express simple properties about objects.

Predicate Calculus An extension of propositional calculus in which the use of quantified variables are permitted.

Problem Domain The collection of knowledge that is needed to solve a specified problem.

Problem Representation The art and science of structuring and representing a problem in the form of a computer program. Problem representation involves defining the necessary algorithms and knowledge structures to solve a problem.

Problem Solving The process of finding solutions to problems by working with goal states and initial states.

Procedural Knowledge Knowledge that can be represented as a procedure or process. Procedural programming languages represent knowledge in the form of algorithms.

Procedural Language A programming language that is based on algorithms. Examples of procedural languages are Pascal, C, BASIC, and FORTRAN.

Production Rule A rule of the IF-THEN format that consists of a premise and conclusion. Production rules are often used in expert systems to represent the knowledge of the expert.

Proposition An expression in which either a true or false statement is made about an object.

Propositional Calculus A formal logic system used to represent the true or false value about objects.

Propositional Logic *See Propositional Calculus.*

Prototyping The technique of building a preliminary version of a program. Prototyping techniques are often employed by expert system developers.

Recursion A technique of defining an object or action in terms of itself. Recursion is frequently used in Turbo Prolog to control the execution of programs.

Recursive Transition Network (RTN) A specialized transition network designed for representing natural languages.

Registers   Storage devices used by augmented transition networks to hold the structural components of a sentence.

Resolution   The inference process used by Turbo Prolog to solve for goals.

Robotics   The branch of engineering and computer science that is involved in developing functional robots.

Rule   A clause that expresses relationships between facts.

Script   A knowledge structure based on the frame representation. Scripts are used to represent sequences of events.

Semantic Network   A general type of knowledge representation in which objects and values are represented as nodes and relations are represented as connections or arcs.

Semantics   The meaning of an expression.

Shallow Knowledge   *See Surface Knowledge.*

Shell   *See Expert System Shell.*

Slot   The storage unit in a frame. Slots contain information such as an object's name, attributes, values, default values, ranges, and references to other frames.

Standard Predicate   A built-in Turbo Prolog predicate. Turbo Prolog provides an extensive library of built-in predicates for performing such operations as I/O, file handling, graphics, and windows.

Start State   The conditions that are assigned at the beginning of a problem.

State Transition Network   *See Transition Network.*

Static Database   A database that does not change during the execution of a program.

Static Knowledge   Knowledge used in a program, such as facts and rules, that does not change.

Sub-goal   Goals that are part of other goals.

Surface Knowledge   Knowledge that is based on the more superficial aspects of a specific topic.

Symbolic Processing   The technique of computing with symbols. Symbolic processing is important to artificial intelligence programs because it is believed that people use symbolic processing techniques to solve problems.

Syntax The structure of an expression.

Term A simple object, compound object, list, or variable.

Token Any term in a string such as a name, number, or non-space.

Transition Network A graph structure used for representing languages and expressions. Transition networks consist of initial states, middle states, and goal states.

Tree A hierarchical structure used to represent both data and knowledge.

Uncertainty *See Certainty Factor.*

Unification The built-in pattern matching technique that Turbo Prolog uses to match the goals and sub-goals in a program.

Variable A name that can be assigned a value. In Turbo Prolog all variables must begin with an uppercase letter.

Vision Systems Computer systems that have the capability to recognize objects in the world.

Voice Recognition Computer systems that can recognize human speech.

Working Memory The memory used in an expert system to store facts and conclusions during the course of a consultation with the system.

Index

A Very Special Offer for People Who <u>Hate</u> to Type!

If you're like most programmers, you'd rather be programming than typing in code from a book. That's right! Typing is a complete waste of time. In fact, that's why we use computers in the first place.

If you want to experiment with and use the programs and utilities developed in this book, there is a better alternative to staying up all night and typing them in. You can now order all of the source code included in this book for just $24.95. Just fill in the order form below and mail it with your payment today.

Send order to:

Keith Weiskamp
Turbo Prolog Disks
3120 E. Paradise Ln., Suite 12
Phoenix, AZ 85032

Please send me _____ copies of The TURBO PROLOG DISK.

☐ Check or money order enclosed for $24.95
(Shipping and handling included)

Name (please print) _____

Title _____ Company _____

Address _____

City _____ State _____ Zip Code _____

Phone Number (daytime) _____
Prices and Terms Subject to Change Without Notice